The Book of Lamentations

The Book of Lamentations

A MEDITATION AND TRANSLATION

David R. Slavitt

The Johns Hopkins University Press

BALTIMORE AND LONDON

© 2001 THE JOHNS HOPKINS UNIVERSITY PRESS
All rights reserved. Published 2001
Printed in the United States of America on acid-free paper

2   4   6   8   9   7   5   3   1

The Johns Hopkins University Press
2715 North Charles Street
Baltimore, Maryland 21218-4363
www.press.jhu.edu

Library of Congress Cataloging-in-Publication Data

Bible. O. T. Lamentations. English.
The book of Lamentations : a meditation and translation /
David R. Slavitt.
p.   cm.
Includes bibliographical references (p.   ).
ISBN 0-8018-6617-0 (pbk)
1. Ninth of Av—Meditations. 2. Jews—History.
I. Slavitt, David R., 1935– II. Title.
BS1533 .S53 2001
224′.305209—dc21   00-010553

A catalog record for this book is available from the British Library.

In memory of my mother and father

Contents

Preface

As we search for answers to our personal problems, some of us find that there can be a kind of solace and encouragement in the suffering of others — or in our observation of how they bore it. Among the most sublime moments of drama, after all, are the deaths of Lear and of Oedipus. My own tribulations — I am almost ashamed to say — have made me, very probably, a better poet and a better reader. I understand some things more deeply. In order to tell the truth, it is sometimes necessary to say the almost unspeakable, but the fact remains that grief has its benefits as well as its costs.

Our modern medical, social, and psychological vocabularies are not well equipped to handle metaphysical and spiritual questions, but it can happen that in one's grief and despair, the world reveals itself in a new aspect, allowing a darker view of the truth of the human condition than one may perhaps have acknowledged — or did acknowledge but could not, until the moment of catastrophe, truly comprehend. This is what I take Aeschylus to mean when he says, in the *Agamemnon*, that "wisdom comes from suffering."

In a culture that has been not only secularized but trivialized, wisdom is in short supply. From moments of joy, we seem regrettably to learn very little. What we discover in agony may not be the only truth but is nonetheless *a* truth—a new, intimate, and unintellectual relationship to the tragedy of the human condition. And wisdom so expensively acquired is not something we are willing to relinquish.

It was my need for comfort during a period of depression that brought me to the Book of Lamentations. I had read and translated Ovid's poetry of exile and some of Seneca's bloody tragedies, but one comes home in the end, and I turned to that masterpiece of grief of my own culture, the *Megillat Eichah*.

I had thought of supplying a brief prose introduction to this biblical text, but my reading and thinking invited—even required—a more carefully considered and well-wrought response. I had what seemed at first the presumptuous idea of trying to match the cadences and diction of Lamentations, but in time that notion seemed less bizarre and even inevitable. Any translation, after all, requires that a poet internalize the source text and reproduce it not only in his own language but also in his own voice and timbre. Having learned that voice as I translated the five chapters of Eichah, how could I not use it to supply the historical background and offer some of my thoughts about the destruction of the Temple and the sufferings of the Exile?

IN JERUSALEM recently on a Thursday morning, I observed a Bar Mitzvah being celebrated at the Kotel—the Wailing Wall—and watched as the officiating rabbi, a hearty, burly man in his seventies, raised the Bar Mitzvah boy up to his shoulders and commenced to dance. I remarked to my daughter-in-law, a rabbinical student, that I simply couldn't understand what the charm was of doing this *here*. Or at Masada, either, for that matter, where people also have Bar Mitzvahs as well as swearing-in ceremonies for the Israeli armed forces.

These are not happy places, I observed, and I said that I'd as soon celebrate such an occasion at Auschwitz.

"Auschwitz isn't ours," she said, after a moment's thought.

After another moment, I answered her: "It is now."

Acknowledgments

The author wishes to express his gratitude to the Open Society Institute's Project on Death in America for its generous support of this undertaking.

Chapter 2 of the Translation of the Book of Lamentations appeared in *Boulevard*.

Note on the Translation

The rendering into English of any text from another language poses a series of impossible problems. A translator wants to be faithful to the original work but then discovers how fidelity to the word can mean a betrayal of the sentence. These difficulties are particularly excruciating with the Book of Lamentations, for the Bible is a venerable, intimidating, and, to many, even a sacred book. How can one dare, even in the name of fidelity, to take liberties? How can one presume to invent?

The question can be turned around, however, for those translations that offer a word-by-word rendition of the Hebrew inevitably miss other aspects of the original that are by no means peripheral. The first four chapters of the book are, in Hebrew, acrostics, the initial letters of their verses running down the twenty-two letters of the Hebrew alphabet. The third is, indeed, a triple acrostic. (The final chapter is not an acrostic, but, inasmuch as it is twenty-two verses long, it echoes what has gone before and can even be taken as a mimetic representation of brokenness or of the silence of God.)

Any version in English that fails, then, to reproduce this curious trope has missed what I take to be an essential aspect of the text, for what we have here is not merely embellishment but a serious assertion that the language itself is speaking, that the speech is inspired, and that there is, beyond all the disaster and pain the book recounts, an intricacy and an orderly coherence the poetry affirms in a gesture that is encouraging and marvelous. The texture of the poetry is what lets us know that, somehow, the catastrophe is not total.

Obviously, to reproduce the acrostics requires a translator to rove a little, to reorder, to adjust. This practice, which I developed in my versions of the Psalms and in some passages in my versions of the Twelve Prophets and of Ibn Gabirol's *A Crown for the King*, I have continued here. My hope is that this practice is not a profanation but rather a demonstration of a kind of faithfulness. Do I worry about what I am doing? Of course, I do. But at moments of doubt, I tell myself that the original text remains and that nothing I have done or can do will hurt it. What I sometimes allow myself to imagine is that there will be some readers for whom my version may be enlightening as they confront—many of them, for the first time—this extraordinary dance of letters and words, which is as close to the heart of the book as the terrible suffering it describes. What I hope is that there may be people who will see in what is here my love for the work and that they may come to feel that love themselves.

PART I

Meditation

1

As a boy, I knew next to nothing of Tish'a b'Av—the Ninth day
of the month of Av—for it comes in the summertime, when
Hebrew schools are closed and children are away at camp. The
destruction of the Temple? That was a very long time ago and
in another country. We were Americans, upbeat, happy people,
looking always on the bright side.

To fast, to go to shul and sit on the floor, unshaven, even un-
showered for God's sake (yes, exactly, for God's sake), mourning for ancient catastrophes? How could parents tell their
children of such observances and explain the terrible truths of
God's rough embrace that has been the life of Jews?

According to Second Kings, the First Temple was burned not on
the ninth of Av but the seventh. And according to Jeremiah,
it was the tenth. But Betar, Bar Kokhba's last stronghold, fell
on the ninth in 135. And all the catastrophes that happened
around that sad date were then ascribed to it.

The expulsion from Spain? That, too. Isaac Abravanel claims that
this happened on the ninth of Av, although that reckoning
may have been off by a couple of days. But the time of the year

3

is right, the Yahr-zeit. And the expulsion from England in 1290. That, too. And the beginning of the deportation of the Jews from Warsaw.

The Tish'a b'Av service includes a reading of dirges, the *qinot* of the *Megillat Eichah*, The Book of Lamentations. There are *qinot* for the massacres of the Crusades, for the Chmielnicki pogrom of 1648, and for the one in Baghdad in 1941. Judah Halevi has an elegy for Zion. And there are *qinot*, now, for the Shoah.

I did not know any of these prayers as a child, but the *qinah* is the only prayer that comes easily to my lips. I cannot even imagine a faith that could follow the instructions of the Seer of Lublin, who said that when Av comes, we diminish joy, but we can diminish Av by rejoicing.

There is a midrash that says the Messiah will be born on Tish'a b'Av, but I fear this is only because grief, if deep enough, will reach out to anything, no matter how far-fetched. Shabbetai Tsevi was said to have been born on Tish'a b'Av. His followers would of course have made such a claim. And his sorry story is one more sadness to ascribe to this woeful day.

The Lubavichers maintain that a descent for the purpose of ascent is not a descent, from which they argue that God's purpose in exiling his people is to elevate us to a higher rung. The destruction of the Temple was the beginning of the process of Redemption. The Lubavichers are as mad as their hatters.

They also point out that Tish'a b'Av always falls on the same day of the week as the first day of Passover, and in this they see a miraculous message: that both holidays point toward redemption. I see miraculous mishegaas. But a small part of me hopes that I am the one who is wrong.

On Tish'a b'Av Jews visit the graves of their departed. Why not? It is a gloomy day anyway. What is there to lose?

I rarely visit my parents' graves. And when I go, I have no idea what to do. They are not there. God is not there, either. There is not even the shimmer of his redolent absence. Hopkins calls out, "Elected Silence, sing to me / And beat upon my whorlèd ear," but as I stand there among the goose droppings that punctuate the grass, my ear picks up nothing at all. I try to take some comfort from the familiar names on the stones — not just my parents' stone, but Uncle Bernie's, which is next to theirs, and others nearby: the Elinsons', Dr. Hecht's, and Rabbi Gelb's.

What I feel for a moment or two is what Thornton Wilder has made it almost impossible to experience in an unliterary way but must have once prompted him to write Our Town — and ruin it for the rest of us, who do not come to a graveyard for literary experience but simply and unembellishedly to mourn.

Literature can be the enemy of honest feeling. At such moments, I
can hate what I do.

When the Lubavichers go to the cemetery to their Rebbe's *ohel*, I
suspect they carry less of a burden of self-consciousness than
I do. They have other burdens, of course: those expensive *strei-
mels*, their fringed garments, their 613 observances. But they
have their faith. They think their Rebbe was the Messiah. I am
not persuaded.

More important, such optimism seems a betrayal of the spirit of
Tish'a b'Av, which is anguish. It is our Good Friday, but there
is no Easter Sunday that follows.

It is forbidden on Tish'a b'Av even to study the Torah, except for
the Book of Job and the Book of Lamentations. This is the
day on which we grieve for every terrible thing that happens
in this world. It is the worst day of the year.

3

There are other, minor fasts, some of which I had never heard of
even in my childhood. There is the Fast of Gedaliah on the
third of Tishrei, which commemorates the murder of Gedaliah ben Ahikam, whom Nebuchadnezzar appointed governor
of Judaea after the destruction of the First Temple. Ishmael
ben Nethaniah, a member of the Jewish royal family, killed
him as a collaborationist — thus ending the last vestige of
Jewish self rule.

There is the Ta'anit Bekhorim, the Fast of the Firstborn, on the
fourteenth of Nisan, the day before Passover, which recalls
how the firstborn Jews were spared while the firstborn Egyptians were dying. When a firstborn is too young to fast, his
father fasts on his behalf.

There is the Ta'anit Esther, the day before Purim. This has fallen
mostly into disuse except among Persian Jews, the twenty-five
thousand or so who are still there.

There is the fast of Shiv'ah Asar be-Tammuz, the seventeenth of
Tammuz, which marks the beginning of the Three Weeks
of Mourning and commemorates the breaching of the walls
of Jerusalem by Nebuchadnezzar in 586 B.C. — which took
place, actually, on the ninth of Tammuz, on which date the
fast was originally observed. But it was on the seventeenth
that Titus breached the walls in 70, and both disasters were
conflated. As disasters tend to be.

On this day, Moses descended from Sinai to find the Golden Calf
and broke the first set of tablets carrying the commandments.
On this day, in the time of the First Temple, the tradition is
that the priests stopped offering the daily sacrifice because of

a shortage of sheep during Nebuchadnezzar's siege, and then, the following year, the walls were breached.

On this day, Pope Gregory IX ordered the confiscation of all copies of the Talmud in 1239. And on this day four thousand Jews were killed in Toledo and Jaen in 1391, and in 1559, the Jewish quarter of Prague was burned. On this day the ghetto in Kovno was liquidated in 1944. On this day in 1970 all Jewish property in Libya was confiscated.

And this is a minor fast, one that lasts only from sunrise to sunset. The major fasts, Yom Kippur and Tish'a b'Av, begin at sunset and continue until the next sunset.

During the seven days of mourning for a death—shivah, which means simply "seven"—the conventional phrase of condolence one offers is "May the Almighty comfort you together with those who mourn for Zion and Jerusalem." Tish'a b'Av is the day when we mourn for Zion and Jerusalem.

4

The Temple—the *Beit HaMikdash,* the Home of the Sanctuary—was
on Mount Moriah, the mountain to which Abraham took
Isaac, his son, to bind him and sacrifice him to the Lord.

This selflessness of Abraham's, this demonstration of his almost
unimaginable obedience and faith in an all but unimaginable
God, is beyond our comprehension. For this reason, when we
pray, we do so not only on our own but invoking Abraham,
our more virtuous and worthier forebear, for whose sake we
implore God to hear our prayers and be merciful to us.

But virtue by association is a dangerous doctrine, for its converse
is guilt by association, so the Diaspora can be seen as punishment for the sins of remote generations against which the
ancient prophets spoke out. Those Jews who suffered during
the Crusades, and the Inquisition, and the Shoah were, in this
view, all being punished for sins of men and women who had
been dead for centuries, for millennia.

Solomon dedicated his Temple to the Lord in 964 B.C., more or
less, announcing that to this place the Lord's eyes would be
open day and night, toward this house, the place where he had
promised to set his name. And he prayed to the Lord that
he would hear the prayers offered in this place and toward
this place.

And we still face the *Beit HaMikdash* when we pray, hoping that from
heaven, his dwelling place, God may remember and keep
Solomon's promise.

Judaism is a religion that cannot quite forget how it used to be a
cult. Abraham broke his father's idols and asserted an ab-

stract God in which, nevertheless, his faith was limitless; when Solomon built the Temple, Abraham's abstraction was reduced not merely to the concrete but to gold and silver and burnished bronze.

Writing much later, in exile, the Kings chronicler put into the mouth of the Lord these words with which he imagined God replying to Solomon: "I have heard your prayer and your supplication, and I have consecrated this house that you have built and put my name there forever. My eyes and my heart will be there for all time. And if you will walk before me as David your father did, with honesty of heart and righteousness, obeying my commandments and keeping my laws and decrees, I will maintain your royal throne over Israel forever, as I promised David your father, when I told him, 'There will always be a man on the throne of Israel.'

"But if you turn away from me, or if your children fail to obey my commandments and keep my laws and decrees, and if they worship other gods, I will cut off Israel from the land I have given them, and the house I have consecrated for my name. Israel will become a proverb and a byword among all peoples, and this fine house will become a heap of ruins.

"And everyone passing by will be astonished and will hiss, and will ask, 'Why has the Lord done this to the land and to this house?' And they will conclude, 'Because they forsook the Lord who brought their fathers out of the land of Egypt, and lay hold of other gods and worshipped them, and served them, and for this reason the Lord has brought all this evil upon them.'" *

* 1 Kings 9.3–9

It is as if the Temple were merely a preparation for the reality we now behold, that remnant, the Wailing Wall, a monument not only to God's glory but also to the brokenness of the world we live in. It is not to the Temple Solomon built but to this ruin the world has made that the words properly apply: "For now I have chosen and consecrated this house, that my name may be there forever; my eyes and my heart will be there for all time." *

* Chronicles 7.16

5

"Zedekiah was the king of Judaea, and in the tenth month Nebuchadnezzar brought his army to besiege Jerusalem, and in the eleventh year of Zedekiah's reign, in the fourth month, on the ninth day, the city walls were breached, and all the princes of the King of Babylon entered the city and sat in the middle gate, including Samgar-nebo, Marshal Sarsechim, General Nergal-sarezer, and all the rest of the potentates of the King of Babylon.

"When King Zedekiah and the soldiers of Judaea saw them, they fled, sneaking out at night through the secret gate in the king's garden and heading for Arabah. But the Chaldeans pursued them and caught them on the plain of Jericho. They brought them back to King Nebuchadnezzar at Riblah, in the land of Hamath, and at Riblah the King of Babylon passed sentence upon them—that the sons of Zedekiah should be slain before the father's eyes, and all the nobles of Judah should be slain as Zedekiah looked on, and then Zedekiah's eyes should be put out, so that those deaths would be the last thing he would ever see.

"And they bound Zedekiah in chains and they carried him off to Babylon. And they burned his palace and the house of the people, and they razed the walls of Jerusalem. And Nebuzaradan, the captain of the Babylonian palace guard, carried away into exile those people who had remained in the city."*

Blinding him that way was unnecessary. Did the Babylonians suppose that there could be any way in which those images would not remain with him for as long as he lived? But blinding was

---

* Jeremiah 39.1–9

the routine punishment for treason, which means there was not even any particular animus.

Was it, as the chronicler says, his fault? "He did what was evil in the sight of the Lord his God. He did not humble himself before Jeremiah the prophet, who spoke from the mouth of the Lord. He also rebelled against King Nebuchadnezzar, who had made him swear by God; he stiffened his neck and hardened his heart against turning to the Lord, the God of Israel."*

Assuming that Zedekiah was guilty as charged and that "the leading priests and the people, likewise were exceedingly unfaithful," what sense does it make for God to do as he did when he "slew [the] young men with the sword in the house of their sanctuary, and had no compassion on young man or virgin, old man or aged; he gave them all into [the] hands [of the king of the Chaldeans]. And all the vessels of the house of God, great and small, and the treasures of the house of the Lord, and the treasures of the king and of his princes, all these he brought to Babylon. And they burned the house of God, and broke down the wall of Jerusalem, and burned all its palaces with fire, and destroyed all its precious vessels."†

Primo Levi tells us that for those who were in the camps, all later experience was merely provisional and untrustworthy. That horror they had experienced remained with them as the truth of their lives forever.

Had King Jehoiachin not refused in 598 B.C. to pay tribute to Nebuchadnezzar, that emperor might not have sent his soldiers the next year to teach the Kingdom of Judaea a lesson in man-

* 2 Chronciles 36.12–13
† 2 Chronicles 36.17–19

13

ners as well as political reality. Jehoiachin was removed and his uncle Zedekiah set on the throne in his place.

Had Zedekiah listened to the prophet Jeremiah and, presumably, other counselors who warned that Babylon was strong and Egypt not to be trusted, he might not have rebelled against Nebuchadnezzar. It was a stupid, mad, and ruinous undertaking.

In a sense, he deserved what he got. There is nothing surprising about what happened, except that we had a covenant with God, in whom we believed.

This was the end of the House of David, which had reigned for four hundred years. And with the death of Gedaliah in Mizpah, just north of Jerusalem, we were no longer Judaeans or Israelites: we had become Jews.

Primo Levi's macabre version of the "Shema":

> Consider that this has been:
> I commend these words to you.
> Engrave them on your hearts
> When you are in your house, when you walk on your way,
> When you go to bed, when you rise.
> Repeat them to your children. Or may your house crumble,
> Disease render you powerless,
> Your offspring avert their faces from you.

Consider that this has been. What he is saying here is not Holocaust theology but Jewish theology, and it always has been.

There is a midrash that tells us that at the destruction of the Temple, God wept and said, "Woe is me! What have I done? I let my Shekhinah dwell below on earth for Israel's sake, but they have sinned and I have returned to my former habitation. I cannot become a laughingstock to the nations and a joke to human kind."

And Metatron, the archangel, came to him and fell on the ground and spoke before the Holy One, saying "Lord of the Universe, let me weep, but you should not weep." And God replied to the archangel, "If you will not let me weep, I shall go to a place where you cannot enter and will weep there, alone, for as it is said, 'But if you will not hear it, my soul shall weep in secret for your pride.' " *

---

* Jeremiah 13.17

6

In 539 B.C., Cyrus, king of Persia, defeated the Babylonian army and
the next year entered Babylon. A benevolent conqueror, he
did not plunder and butcher or raze the city but, on the contrary, brought peace and harmony. On a clay cylinder that
has survived, he declares: "My troops wandered peacefully
throughout Babylon. In all Sumer and Akkad I let no man be
afraid . . . The dwellers in Babylon . . . I freed from the yoke
that ill became them. I repaired their houses, I healed their af-
flictions . . . I am Cyrus, king of all, the great king, the mighty
king, king of Babylon, king of Sumer and Akkad, king of the
four corners of the earth."

He was tolerant of the local religions and restored the daily worship
of Marduk, the city's chief god. On that cylinder, he boasts,
"I brought the gods back into their sanctuaries."

His tolerance extended to the Jews, whom he allowed to return to
Jerusalem. Their property that Nebuchadnezzar had plundered he restored.

But after fifty years in Babylon, and with a benevolent king now on
the throne of a rich and peaceful city, was it a blessing or a
burden to make the eight-hundred-mile-long trip back to a
ruined homeland?

In Ezra we read how the first wave of Jews returned from their
exile led by Sheshbazzar, a prince of Judah and probably a
member of the house of David. The name is close enough
so that he might have been Shenazar, the fourth son of King
Jehoiachin.

In the spring of 537 B.C., fifty thousand Jews, more or less, set out
for Jerusalem. They had, as Ezra tells us and as Nehemiah
confirms, 736 horses, 245 mules, 435 camels, and 6,720 asses.

For a part of the trip, they followed the route Abraham had taken
fourteen hundred years before.

They began the rebuilding of the Temple, but life was not easy in
this barren land, and they left it unfinished. Haggai nagged
that they should build the Lord's house, but they were poor
and had to make a living. They needed roofs over their own
heads.

In 530 B.C. Cyrus died, and his son Cambyses II succeeded him.
Cambyses conquered Egypt and made Persia the greatest
empire the world had yet seen, extending from the Indus to
the Nile.

It was during the reign of his son Darius that Zerubbabel and
Jeshua resumed the work of rebuilding the Temple, and they
completed the reconstruction on the third day of Adar, in the
sixth year of Darius's reign, or 517 B.C.

It was the same size as Solomon's Temple and had the same ground
plan, with the Holy of Holies, the Sanctuary with the Golden
Altar, and the table lampstand and other furnishings. This
was surrounded by an inner court with an altar for burnt
offerings and an outer court. But it was not the same, for the
Talmud tells us that five elements were lacking: the Ark; the
sacred fire; the Shekhinah; the Holy Spirit; and the Urim and
Thummim.

It was a copy and therefore dedicated not merely and directly to
God but to the memory of the First Temple. Rebuilt on the

site of a ruin, it lacked the assurance and joy of the original. Its Eternal Light, which had been extinguished and relit, was now so called more in hope than in reason.

Darius expressly confirmed the permission Cyrus had given the Jews to worship in their way and rebuild the Temple. Clerks rummaged through the files in Ecbatana, the summer capital of Media, and found the old records, and Darius ordered Tattenai, governor of the Province Beyond the River, to allow Zerubbabel to complete his work on the building and "let the work of this house of God alone." *

But permission that comes from a king can be revoked by that king or another. The Persians lost at Marathon in 491 B.C. and at Salamis in 480. And at Issus in 333, Alexander the Great defeated Darius III, and the edicts and judgments of the kings of Persia were of no further consequence or meaning.

* Ezra 6.6

7

Were the people holy because of the Temple, or was it the other way around, that the Temple was sacred because of the people?

Who can even imagine the Holy of Holies, within which stood the Ark, shrouded in darkness: because for anyone to see it would be instantly fatal? An abstract god may be hard to love, but did this chest of acacia wood covered with gold make it easier? Was this a trinket, a souvenir of Moses' encounter with the Lord? Or had it become, itself, an object of worship, a substitution for the invisible God and therefore a rival?

Were the tablets of Sinai in it? Or the copy text of the Torah?

Moses reportedly gave us thirteen Torahs, one for each of the tribes and the canonical text on deposit in the Ark of the Temple. But this is a later version of the story, a conflation of the Ark and the Azarah, the Temple courtyard, where the official Torah might well have been kept.

In the Second Temple, instead of the Ark, there was still God's holy vessel, the congregation with whom he had made the Covenant. And they knew now that the terms of that agreement could be enforced and that God's love was conditional and his mercy not without limit. For as Moses had said to them many years before: "If you will not obey the voice of the Lord God or be careful to obey his commandments and statutes I have given you this day, then all these curses shall befall you and overtake you. Cursed shall you be in the city and cursed in the field. Cursed shall be your basket and your kneading trough. Cursed shall be the fruit of your body and the fruit of your fields, the increase of your cattle and the young of your flocks. Cursed shall you be at your coming in and at your going out.

"The Lord will send down on you curses, confusion, frustration in all that you try to do, until you are destroyed and you perish directly because of the evil of your actions, because you have forsaken me. The Lord will make the pestilence cling to you until he has consumed you from the land you are entering and are about to possess. The Lord will afflict you with consumption, fever, inflammation, and thirst, and the heavens over your head shall be brass and the earth beneath your feet shall be iron. The Lord will make the rain of your land powder and dust, and from heaven it shall come down upon you until you are destroyed utterly." [*]

There are those who read in these verses a prediction of the ashes in the skies that floated down from the crematoria of Auschwitz and Birkenau.

A God who reveals himself in history is easy to fear but difficult to love. And the sorry history of the Jews is all there in Moses' litany of threats: "You shall become a horror, a proverb, and a byword among the peoples into whose lands the Lord will lead you[†] . . . You shall carry much seed into the field but shall gather little, for the locust shall eat it. You shall plant vineyards and dress the vines, but you shall not drink the wine nor gather the grapes, for the worm will consume them. You shall have olive trees throughout your lands, but you shall not anoint yourself with the oil, for your olives shall drop off the branches.

"You shall beget sons and daughters but they shall not be yours, for they shall be led away into captivity. And all your trees and the fruit of your ground the locust shall possess. The so-

[*] Deuteronomy 28.15–24
[†] Deuteronomy 28.25

journer who is among you shall mount above you higher and higher and you shall come down lower and lower. He shall lend to you and you shall not lend to him. He shall be the head and you shall be the tail. All these curses shall come down on you and pursue you and overwhelm you until you are destroyed because you did not obey the voice of the Lord your God to keep his commandments and his statutes. They shall be upon you as a sign and a wonder, on you and your descendants forever." *

It is difficult to read these verses without thinking of the Diaspora and of the Shoah: "Whereas you were as the stars of the heavens for multitude, you shall be left few in number because you did not obey the voice of the Lord your God. And as the Lord took delight in doing you good, so the Lord will take delight in bringing ruin upon you and destroying you. And you shall be plucked off the land which you are entering and about to possess. And the Lord will scatter you among all the peoples from one end of the earth to the other, and there you shall serve other gods, of wood and stone, which neither you nor your fathers have known. And among these nations you shall find no ease, and there shall be no rest for the sole of your foot, but the Lord will give you there a trembling heart and failing eyes and a languishing soul. Your life shall hang in doubt before you. Night and day, you shall be in dread and you shall live always in doubt. In the morning, you shall say, 'Would that it were evening!' and in the evening you shall say 'Would that it were morning!' because of the fear in your heart and the horrors before your eyes." †

* Deuteronomy 28.38–46
† Deuteronomy 28.62–67

21

This is unreasonable and absurd. But it happened, just as Moses said it would. And we are forced to choose between absolute meaninglessness and the even more dreadful possibility of meaning. Can we suppose that the anger and jealousy of the Lord did this? Was it all our fault?

"Then men would say, 'It is because they forsook the covenant of the Lord, the God of their fathers, which he made with them when he brought them out of the land of Egypt, and they went and served other gods and worshiped them, gods whom they had not known and whom he had not allotted to them. Therefore the anger of the Lord was kindled against this land, bringing upon it all the curses written in this book." *

And the Enlightenment, in which we believed? (In which I believed!) There are those who would say that it, too, was a false god.

---

* Deuteronomy 29.24–26

8

The Persians had been tolerant, as was Alexander, whom Josephus
reports to have come to Jerusalem to sacrifice at the Temple,
where Jaddua the High Priest received him with great pomp.
It might have happened, or it could have been Parmenion, his
general. Alexander was occupied with the conquest of Tyre
and Gaza and was on his way to Egypt.

At Alexander's death, his generals divided the empire among themselves, Egypt going to Ptolemy, Syria to Seleucus, and Greece
and Macedon to Antigonus. Then, for generations, they
fought one another, each of them wanting it all.

What they failed to notice was the threat from the west: the Romans
were coming who would take it all for themselves and rule
the world.

For the first hundred years, the land of the Jews was part of the
Ptolemaic holdings, and we lived well, learning from the
Greeks, whom it was impossible not to admire. Aeschylus,
Sophocles, Euripides, Phidias, Plato, Aristotle, and Pericles
are admirable men—or, one might say, seductive.

Some Jews moved to Alexandria, which was a rich and splendid city.
Thousands and then tens of thousands of Jews moved there,
were welcomed, and lived there in comfort. Their children
spoke and thought in Greek. And prayed in Greek, for they
had forgotten Hebrew and needed a translation of the Torah
into Greek.

But in 195 B.C. Antiochus the Great defeated Ptolemy V at a battle
at the Jordan and took Judah as his prize, and it became a part
of the Seleucids' territory.

But the Romans defeated Antiochus at Thermopylae in 191 B.C. and
at Magnesia in 190, and they exacted from him all his lands
west of the Taurus mountains and much tribute.

His son Antiochus IV, called Epiphanes, had to pay the tribute, too,
and he got it from the people over whom he ruled, including,
of course, the Jews.

It was simony, or bribery, or simply general business practice, but a
way of making money from the Jews was to accept gifts from
those who wanted to be High Priest — Onias III, or, later on,
Onias's brother Jason. And three years after that, he removed
Jason and appointed Menelaus.

Each of these High Priests used the wealth of the Temple to repay
Antiochus for his kindnesses. Antiochus eventually figured
out that he didn't need these middlemen: it would be more
efficient if he simply plundered the Temple, himself.

In 167 he looted the Temple, abolished the reading of the Torah, the
observance of the Sabbath, and even circumcision. Possession
of a Torah scroll was punishable by death.

The walls of Jerusalem were razed, and foreigners settled in the new
citadel he built amidst the ruins.

And then comes the story I knew, the story of Hanukkah, of
Mattathias, and Judah Maccabee, and his brother Jonathan,
and the purification of the Temple, and the oil — or was it
naphtha? — that lasted for the miraculous eight days.

But if the story we tell our children stops here, the history con-
tinues, and in 143 Jonathan is murdered, and his brother Simon
takes over as High Priest, and then, at his death, his son
John Hyrcanus, who issues coinage, as if he were a king, and

forcibly converts the Edomites to Judaism. And when John's
son Aristobulus I succeeds him, he declares himself king.

At the death of Aristobulus, his brother Alexander Yannai ascends
to the throne and expands the kingdom, but after him, his
wife, Salome Alexandra, rules, and at her death in 67 B.C. their
sons, Aristobulus II and Hyrcanus II, fight it out about who
should be the ruler . . .

It's not worth fighting about. The people are Hellenized, as the
names of these Hasmonean rulers make clear. The religion
is breaking up into sects and cults. And in any event, the
Romans are coming.

In 63 B.C. they arrive, and they can name whomever they want to
rule what they call the province of Judaea.

9

The Zealots brought on the Jewish War of A.D. 66 to 70, a faction of radical priests, Jewish ayatollahs to whom I can feel no connection. Along with them were the Sicarii, a band of fanatics who went about with daggers under their cloaks and talked of throwing off the yoke of Rome. These people were as mad as the rebels against Babylon and even more stupid, because they ought to have known what could happen: it had happened before.

Not once but many times. The Second Temple that Antiochus IV had looted and desecrated and that Judah Maccabee had reconsecrated in 165, King Herod the Great rebuilt. He completed the work in A.D. 63 and made it one of the most impressive structures of the Roman empire, extending the Temple Mount as well, filling in much of the Valley of the Cheesemakers, and installing the retaining walls made of courses of those huge ashlars we see today. The "Western Wall"—the Kotel—was not part of the Temple itself but only of one of those retaining walls of the enlarged hillside beneath it.

Herod built the palace and the citadel at Masada, too. What he achieved on the Temple Mount and at Masada was impressive as architecture and astonishing as engineering. But these monuments, both of them, turned out to be unlucky.

One would think that some of these Hellenized Jews would have understood that grandeur, beyond a certain point, is arrogance and invites disaster.

If it was an invitation, it did not take long before there was a response. Herod's Temple stood only seven years.

In 66, when Florus the Roman procurator demanded seventeen talents of gold from the Temple treasury, there was an uprising in which Rome's garrison was overrun and the Zealot rebels took Jerusalem. This rebellion spread quickly to other cities.

Florus asked for help from the governor of Syria, Caius Cestius Gallus, who came with a legion of soldiers. One riot, one legion. But the rebels inflicted heavy losses on the Roman soldiers, who were forced to withdraw.

The Jews supposed then that they could succeed, not because they doubted the emperor's power but because they believed that God, king of the universe, was more powerful and would protect them. Nero sent Vespasian to deal with them. He came with his son Titus and three of the best legions in the Roman army, attacked from the north, and by October of 67 had taken Iotapata and subdued all of Galilee. Tiberias surrendered to him, but Tarichea did not, and he conquered it and demonstrated to the Jews the cruelty with which Romans could treat those who opposed them.

10

The Roman legions were about to resume their campaign when
word arrived that Nero had committed suicide. Galba succeeded him. Galba was killed, and Otho succeeded him. Vitellius marched down to Rome from Germany with his legions
to defeat Otho's forces and assume the purple.

Vitellius ate four or five meals a day and then vomited so that he
could eat more. His brother Lucius once gave him a banquet
with two thousand different dishes of fish and seven thousand
of poultry. Even Rome was disgusted.

Vespasian was proclaimed emperor by the Roman soldiers in Alexandria on July first of 69. He left his son Titus to continue the
war against the Jews and returned to Italy to burn Cremona
and then storm Rome, where Emperor Vitellius was hiding
under his bed like a terrified child.

Soldiers found him, dragged him out from under the bed and
paraded him naked through the streets with his hands tied
behind him. One of the soldiers held a sword blade under his
chin to make him lift his head. He was then beaten to death
and his head was cut off and stuck on a pole. His trunk was
dragged on a hook to the Tiber and thrown into the river.

These were the Romans who were about to destroy the second
Temple. They were not paragons of virtue. They were not
"God's rod," which he was using to chastise Israel. They were
only very rich and very well organized—as everyone else in
the world at that time understood perfectly well.

It could be argued that the Jews so much believed in heaven and
the power of the Temple that they forgot for the moment

the earth they walked on and the power of armies. It was for this theological error—or call it an act of utter folly and mad pride—that the Temple was destroyed.

Jeremiah had warned them, telling them not to rely on what the priests had been saying. "Do not trust in these deceptive words: 'this is the House of God, the House of God, the House of God.' "* The priests had him arrested and wanted to have him killed for prophesying against the city.

Jacob lay down on the earth and put his head on a pillow, and then awoke to realize that this was a holy place, none other than a house of God and the gate of heaven. Israel, on the Temple Mount, believed that they were in a holy place where God was and believed therefore that they were invulnerable and that he would protect them.

They were dreaming, and for two millennia we have had rocks for our pillows, for this is none other than the earth, and it is the gate of hell.

* Jeremiah 7.4

11

In 70, Titus moved against Jerusalem with the Fifth, Tenth, Twelfth,
and Fifteenth Legions and twenty cohorts of auxiliaries as
well as forces that had been supplied to him from dependent
monarchs—probably eighty thousand men. Against these, the
Jews had twenty-four thousand trained soldiers and a number
of irregular volunteers, and they were at a further disadvantage
because it was Passover, and there were pilgrims and tourists,
hundreds of thousands of them, and the city was so crowded
that it was difficult to maneuver.

From the defeats of Galilee and Samaria, many soldiers had come
to the city to make a last stand, and their presence tipped
the political balance against the moderates and in favor of the
Zealots, whose leader, Eleazar, urged them on to seize the
noblemen and the priests and kill them. What had started out
as an organized although desperate defense was now pretty
much a disorderly mob that seized the Temple and proclaimed
that the Lord was their leader and that they were invincible.

Eleazar must, nonetheless, have had some doubts, for he sent mes-
sages to the Jewish communities in Alexandria, Ctesiphon,
Seleucia, and elsewhere asking for aid. But no help was forth-
coming.

Under the pressure of the attack, the Zealots split into three fac-
tions: Eleazar's extremists; a less violent group led by John of
Giscala; and the force Simon Bargiora brought with him from
Galilee into the city to help defend the ramparts.

Eleazar was assassinated, and John and Simon quarreled about who
should be in command of the defense against the Romans.

Titus called on the Jews to surrender. The Zealots and the moderates debated this question—as if it were a question.

The prayers of Tish'a b'Av assume that God was punishing Judaea for its sins and are full of contrition and the promise that we will try to do better. What is missing is any note of blame for those Zealots who refused the Romans' offer. They could see that there was no hope of surviving the onslaught of such a force.

Titus interrupted the attack to parade his troops before the walls of Jerusalem in order to make it clear to any reasonable person that there was no alternative. The Romans, Josephus tells us, "marched in their thousands and tens of thousands with trumpets blaring, for four days from sunup to sundown, and the ground shook with their footsteps."

The Jews crowded together on the north side of the Temple on the wall and on the rooftops and spat at the Romans. They drove off Titus's envoys with arrows. It was for this as much as anything else that he destroyed Jerusalem.

12

Josephus addressed the Jews,* speaking for the Romans but saying what was clearly the truth: "It would be a Scandalous Bondage in deed to serve a Master that a Man of Honour would be ashamed to own; but it is Another Case to be Subject to a People that have the whole World at their Feet. And where is that Spot in the Universe that has scap'd the Dominion of the Romans; saving only where Extreme Heats or Colds have render'd the Place Intolerable and Useless. Fortune is effectually gone over to them; and the Great Disposer of Empires Himself hath in his Providence at present made Italy the Seat of the Universal Monarch.

"Besides, that is according to the Sovereign Law of Nature that governs in Beasts as well as in Men, to give way to the Stronger and to submit to the Longer Sword. This was it that made your Ancestors, tho' in Power and Politiques much your Superiours, to pay an Allegiance to the Romans: which they would never have done if they had not been thoroughly convinc'd that it was GOD's Will to have it so.

"But to what End is it for you now to dispute a Point any longer, that's as good as Lost already? For if the Walls were yet Entire, and the Siege rais'd, Famine Alone would do the Work. It has begun with the Multitude; and the Soldiers Turn will be Next; and Every Day still worse than the Other; For the Calamity is Insuperable, and there is no Fence against Hunger.

---

* I have retained the orthography and punctuation of the Roger L'Estrange translation of 1709 because I like its elegant remoteness and formality, which somehow suggests Josephus's Greek.

Wherefore you should do well to bethink yourselves in Time, and to take Wholesom Advice before it be too Late."

Indeed, in the besieged city, supplies were running low and people were starving. In an ancient commentary we read how the Romans brought kids that they roasted in their camp to the west of the city so that the winds would bring the smell of the food to the Jews, rousing their appetites so that they died.

It is said that during the destruction of the First Temple the Jews were reduced to eating thistles, but this time there were not even thistles.

After dark, the desperate Jews would sneak out through subterranean passages or climb over the walls to forage for something to eat. The Romans captured these people and crucified them within sight of the stubborn defenders, five hundred of them a day until the hillside was a forest of crosses. And then the Romans ran out of wood to make into crosses.

The stench was terrible. But even this display did not bring the Jews to their senses. On the contrary, because they were terrified of what the Romans would do, it hardened their resolve.

It is too late to blame them for their pride and their fear. It is beside the point to point out how great a mistake they were making. At this distance, such details are indistinguishable and all we can see is a generality that we take for destiny. The carnage was terrible and terribly familiar.

Josephus reports: "When the Temple was now aflame, the Soldiers took all that came to hand, and kill'd all they met, to the Degree of a most Prodigious Slaughter and Pillage: Without any Respect either to Age or Sex; but Young and Old, Sacred and

Prophane, Priests and Laiques, they all were together, and
Men of all Sorts and Qualities were equally involv'd in the
Common Calamities of the War. And whether they Resisted
or Submitted; whether they stood it out or begg'd Quarter,
they far'd all alike. As the Fire advanced, the Crackling of
the Flames was heard in Company with the Dying Groans of
People at their Last Gasp; and betwixt the Depths of the Hill
and the Extent of the Conflagration, the Whole City seem'd
to be but one Continu'd Blaze.

"The Tumult and Uproar was so Dreadful that it is not possible
to imagine any Thing more Terrible: What with the Raging
Outcries of the Roman Legions; the Howling of the Rebels
when they found themselves at the Mercy of Fire and Sword;
and the Dismal Lamentations of Distressed Wretches in the
Temple, betwixt the Enemy and the Fire. In fine, Those upon
the Mountain and those in the City, answering one another by
turns: The Flames Opening the Eyes of those that the Famine
had well nigh Clos'd, and inspiring Fresh Spirit and Ability to
deplore their Misfortunes.

"The Neighbouring Mountains and Places beyond Jordan, Echo-
ing the same Complaints and Grievances over and over again;
and the Calamity, in Weight and Substance, yet more than
the Noise. The flames were so Impetuous and Violent that
the very Mountain the Temple stood upon looked as if it
had been One Body of Fire from the Bottom; and the Bloud,
in Proportion, Answerable to the Flame; for the Number of
the Slain was superior to that of those that did the Execu-
tion. The Ground was cover'd all over with Carcasses, and the
Soldiers pursue'd the Living over the Bodies of the Dead."

13

Even in the time of the Second Temple, the Jews observed the fast of Tish'a b'Av to mourn not only the destruction of the First Temple but also their realization that the Second Temple or any other Temple could be destroyed.

Shabbat Hazon comes just before or just after Tish'a b'Av, or sometimes on that very date, in which case the observance of the fast is deferred to the next day. *Hazon* means "vision," and, according to Reb Hillel of Paritch, on this day God gives every Jew a vision of the Third Temple.

These rabbis are always looking on the bright side. That, perhaps, is the difference between intelligence and faith. But when intelligence tells us one thing and faith tells us another, which should we trust?

We mourn for the Temple, but more than the wood and stone, we mourn for the loss of the Beit HaMikdash, the place in which God was present, His dwelling place on earth. One of the names of God is Hamakom, which means, simply, *the place.* That was the place of *the place.*

During the time that the Temple stood, no one in Jerusalem went to bed at night feeling bereft.

Now there are pious Jews who arise from their beds at midnight and sit on a low stool in the manner of mourners to recite the prayer that the Temple may be rebuilt.

The destruction of the Temple then was as bad as the expulsion from Eden, or worse even, because Adam and Eve did not have to stay there and see how different everything was, how terribly diminished and defiled. They fell from Eden into the world. At the destruction of the Temple, it was the world itself that fell.

In a shul, when one leaves the sanctuary to go to the toilet, one takes off his tallis, which should not be worn in an unclean place. The Temple was the earth's sanctuary; the rest, as we read in the *Mekilta de Rabbi Ishmael,* was unclean: "Before the land of Israel had been especially chosen, all lands were suitable for divine revelations; after the land of Israel had been chosen, all other lands were eliminated. Before Jerusalem had been especially selected, the entire land of Israel was suitable for altars; after Jerusalem had been selected, all the rest of the land of Israel was eliminated. 'Take heed that you do not offer your burnt offerings in every place that you see, but in the place which the Lord shall choose.'* Before the Temple had been especially selected, the whole of Jerusalem was appropriate for the manifestation of the divine presence; after the Temple had been selected, the rest of Jerusalem was eliminated."†

The Haftarah of Tish'a b'Av morning is from Jeremiah,** who says: "The Lord our God has doomed us; he has made us drink a bitter draft, because we have sinned against the Lord. We hoped for good fortune, but no happiness came; we looked for relief, but instead there is terror."

Jeremiah also says: "For the mountains I undertake weeping and wailing, for the pastures of the woodlands, a dirge. They are laid waste and no man passes through; no sound of cattle is heard. The birds of the sky and the beasts too have fled. I will

---

* Deuteronomy 12.14
† Tractate Pischa 42–50
** 9.14–23

turn Jerusalem into rubble, into dens for jackals, and in Judah
there will be ghost towns, desolate and abandoned.

He says: "Death has come up to our windows and has entered
our palaces, cutting off the children from the streets and
the young men from the squares. Thus says the Lord: 'The
corpses of men shall fall like dung upon the open field, like
sheaves after the reaper, and none shall gather them.' "

The Haftarah for the afternoon service from Isaiah is what we
read on all fast days and is mostly cautionary:* "Seek the Lord
while he may be found, call upon him while he is near; let the
wicked forsake his way, and the man of iniquity his thoughts;
and let him return unto the Lord and he will have compassion
upon him, and to our God, for he will abundantly pardon . . ."

That seems too easy. The torment has been going on for too long
to be a question of divine correction of human weakness and
inattention. There is a text in Deuteronomy that is more
closely apposite and also more stern, to explain why the Jews
had to wander forty years in the desert on their way back
from Egypt to the Promised Land: "And you shall remember
all the way which the Lord your God has led you these forty
years in the wilderness, to humble you, and to prove you, to
know what was in your heart, whether you would keep his
commandments or no."†

That has been our history for these two thousand years. And that
is perhaps why some orthodox Jews disapprove of the state of
Israel: because it severs a bond that may have been unpleasant

* 55.6–56.8
† 8.2

37

and even agonizing but was, nonetheless, a connection. The choice is a hard one: to acknowledge an abusive parent or to run away and become, in effect, an orphan.

14

The destruction of the Second Temple was the end of a kind of Judaism with which we feel almost no connection. Animal sacrifices? Priests? These bloody rites are too primitive, too pagan, no different from what the Greeks and the Romans did.

Now, instead of the sacrifice, we have Shacharit and Mincha, which are offerings of prayers in the mornings and in the afternoons.

According to legend, Rabbi Johanan ben Zakkai, who had opposed the war against Rome, was smuggled out of the city by pretending to be dead and having his disciples carry him in a coffin through the Roman lines as if to bury him outside the city.

Legend tells us that he came before Vespasian, who was well impressed by his bravery and his wisdom and who knew, furthermore, that this rabbi had spoken out against the war. The Roman commander let him go on his way and gave him permission to establish a school in Yavneh. The trouble with this story is that Vespasian did not besiege Jerusalem; it was Titus who did this.

But the legend has power because it figures the death and the rebirth of Judaism, for now in the place of priests, there would be rabbis, and instead of the Temple with its bloody altars, there would be synagogues, assemblies, in which, on the bimahs, there would be our new cult object—the Torah itself.

What Rabbi Johanan had been saying, we now know to be true— that the Jews did not really need the city, or the Temple, or even political sovereignty, but that with the Torah alone, we could survive.

We are the People of the Book, and this is the book.

In shuls, on Shabbat mornings, after they open the ark, they parade
the Torah through the congregation, and with our tallis
fringes or the corners of our prayerbooks, we touch the scroll
cover and then kiss what touched that sacred book. There
are prayers, too, of course, but these kisses are the most basic
representation of our love for this great treasure.

This is the moment, on Shabbat mornings, in which my heart reli-
ably opens and I can feel my eyes brim with tears.

The religion we can recognize as ours begins here. Powerless, we had
the power of the Torah, and stateless, we nonetheless had its
laws and statutes.

In the synagogue, each Jew is the high priest of his heart's temple.
Our rabbis are our teachers and masters, but they do not inter-
cede for us, and their prayers are no different from ours. We
do not need or want any priestly caste to stand between us and
our God.

15

One would suppose that the Jews would have learned their lesson in
history's strict school. What they learned was the wrong lesson—that if the Temple could be destroyed, it could also be
rebuilt—from which they concluded that because it had been
rebuilt once after seventy years, this would inevitably happen
again, and in another seventy years there would be another
Temple.

They calculated that by 140, their deliverance would come not only
from Rome but from vicissitude itself. A leader would appear,
a Messiah, and an end to their tribulations.

Or, no, not *a* Messiah, but the real one, whose coming would dis-
prove the Nazarenes' belief in Jeshua.

In 131, Hadrian, passing through on his way to Egypt, declares that
he will build on Jerusalem's rubble a new city, Aliea Capito-
linus, in which he will erect a temple to Jupiter. The Jews are
to be brought into the community of Romans. Tineius Rufus,
governor of the region, has banned circumcision, which the
Romans consider a barbaric practice.

Simon Bar Kosiba raises a rebellion and Rabbi Akiba declares that
this man is the son of a star, from the verse in Numbers about
how a star—a *kokhba*—shall rise out of Jacob and a scepter
from Israel to smite the corners of Moab and destroy the
children of Seth.

Bar Kosiba becomes Bar Kokhba and Akiba's disciples rally around
him, thousands and even hundreds of thousands.

Bar Kokhba, or, as his enemies call him, Bar Koziba, the son of lies.

There is at first some success and, over the course of three and a half years in a guerilla campaign that puzzles the Romans, Bar Kokhba pushes two Roman legions back, reclaims much of Judaea, and even retakes the rubble that remains of Jerusalem. Bar Kokhba mints coins inscribed "to the freedom of Jerusalem."

Hadrian orders Julius Severus to deal with the Jews. This general had put down the Britons' revolt, and now he comes with seven legions to restore order. To reassert reality. The strength of a legion is 6,100 men.

One after another, Bar Kokhba's strongholds fall as bit by bit the Romans retake territory and starve the enclaves of Jews into submission. The last of these redoubts is Betar, near Nazareth. There are said to have been four hundred synagogues within its walls. Betar may have been Sepphoris, a Roman winter camp, or *castra vetera*, that Bar Kokhba had retaken and made his stronghold.

Severus besieges it. There is a secret passage by which Betar is supplied with food and water, and the story is that a traitor showed the Romans the entrance to that tunnel. Either there was a traitor or the Jews had been deluded in the first place. But these possibilities are not mutually exclusive.

In any event, Betar fell — on Tish'a b'Av. The men were killed and the women and children sold as slaves. There were so many slaves on the market all at once that their price fell and a slave was worth less than a horse.

Hadrian banned the study of the Torah, the observance of the Sabbath, and, of course, circumcision. Violation of these prohibitions was punishable by death. The ordination of new

rabbis was also punishable by death. Villages were burnt to
the ground and fruit trees and vineyards cut down. In Galilee,
famous for its olives, not a single tree was left standing.

Rabbi Akiba, Rabbi Ishmael, Rabbi Chanania ben Teradion, and
seven more of their colleagues defied the prohibition, and
Tineius Rufus condemned them all to death. Akiba's death
is famous: he was flayed alive and expired pronouncing the
Shema, extending the vowel of the last word so as to die with
that prayer on his lips.

Tu b'Av—the fifteenth of Av—is a day on which pious Jews rejoice,
for on that day the Jews of Betar were at last permitted to
bury their dead.

Rome had won and the exile had begun, a time of grief and longing
that would stretch out for generations, centuries, millennia.
Clutching a book and the dream of return, we would learn
to live with a God that was everywhere. The earth gods were
the ones we had left behind—Baal, Asherah, Astarte, and
those other local deities against whom the prophets cried and
warned us.

Their blandishments were behind us and we could no longer be
seduced by their wiles. What can the configuration of a moun-
taintop mean to us if it is not our mountain? How can we
experience rapture at a sunset or respond to the sweet sug-
gestion of a sea breeze if the sun sets on an alien landscape or
the breeze blows in from a harbor not our own? The buds of a
new season? The young lambs of a new spring? These are the
riches of an earth that is not ours, except as a way station, a
transit lounge.

16

And in Europe, in England, King Edward I fulfilled every requirement of Pope Honorius in the fight against usury, having
already borrowed from the Jews enough money to keep the
government operating, whether or not the Barons were forth-
coming.

The usury was only a part of it; the rest was hatred, pure and
simple. The *Statutum de Judaismo,* which prohibited the lending
of money at interest, also extended to women the requirement
that Jews wear badges of distinction upon their garments, and
changed the color from white to yellow. In his *History and An-
tiquities of the Jews in England,* D'blossiers Tovey wondered in 1738:
"What mystery there was in thus changeing the Colour of
their Badges I can't guess; unless White was consider'd as an
Emblem of too great Purity and Yellow substituted to denote
Envy and Malice."

The Jews had been so far impoverished under Henry III that there
was almost nothing left to squeeze out of them. But what they
left behind would go into the king's coffers.

Tovey poses this question: "Did the Forefathers of this miserable
People, think you, meet with more rigorous Taskmasters in
Aegypt? They were only call'd upon to make Brick: But nothing less than makeing Gold seems to have been expected from
the Jews in England.

The act of Expulsion was promulgated by King Edward in Council
on July 18, 1290, which was Tish'a b'Av. It ordered all Jews to be
gone by the Feast of All Saints—November 1. Most of them
left on St. Denys' Day, October 9. Their number is said to

have been somewhere between fifteen and seventeen thousand. Matthew of Paris gives the figure as 16,511.

A story from Tovey's account, which he had from Lord Coke: "He says that the richest of the Jewes having imbark'd themselves, with their treasure, in a tall Ship of great Burthen; when it was under Sail and gotten down the Thames, towards the Mouth of the River, beyond Quinborough, the Master of it, confederating with some of the Mariners, invented a Stratagem to destroy them. And to bring the same to pass, commanded to cast Anchor, and rode at the same time till the Ship, at low Water, lay upon the Sands; and then, pretending to walk on the Shore for his health and Diversion, invited the Jews to go along with him; which they, nothing suspecting, readily consented to; and continu'd there till the Tide began to come in again: which as soon as the Master perceiv'd, he privily stole away and was drawn up into the Ship, as had been before concerted.

"But the Jews, not knowing the Danger, continue'd to amuse themselves as before. Till at length, observing how fast the Tide came in upon them, they crowded all the Ship Side, and call'd out for Help. When he, like a Profane Villain, instead of giving them Assistance, scoffingly made Answer that they ought rather to call upon Moses, by whose Conduct their Fathers past thro' the Red Sea, and who was still able to deliver them out of those rageing Floods which came in upon them: and so, without saying any more, leaving them to the Mercy of the Waves, they all miserably perished."

The captain and his officers were hanged, but that did not bring the Jews back to life or to England, to which we were not readmitted until 1656.

17

England was not alone in its harsh treatment of Jews. In France, in Blois, a Christian servant said that he had seen a Jew throw a corpse of a child into the Loire. No corpse was ever found, but the forty Jews who lived in Blois were all imprisoned.

What complicated this business was that Count Thibaut was having an affair with a Jewish woman named Polcelina, and the countess was jealous, and the other Christians, who resented Polcelina's influence at court, conspired to bring about the destruction of all the Jews.

The servant was subjected to an ordeal by water, but he insisted on the truth of his story and his testimony was declared to be true. The Jews were offered the choice of baptism or death. They assumed this was merely a new version of the extortions with which they were familiar, and they attempted to bribe their way out of their predicament, but the mood in Blois had turned ugly. Most of the Jews, including Polcelina, chose death, and on the 26th of May, 1171, thirty-two Jews, seventeen of them women, were burned at the stake.

Rabbenu Tam — Rabbi Jacob Tam — declared the day, the 20th of Sivan, a perpetual fast, "greater than the Fast of Gedaliah, for it is a day of atonement." But it was the Christians of Blois who needed atonement, not the Jews.

It was the Book of Esther but without the reversal at the end. Ephraim of Bonn wrote a "Lament for the Massacre at Blois" in which he complained: "I am stoned, I am struck down, I am crucified, I am burned, my neck is broken in shame, I am beheaded, I am trampled for my guilt, I am strangled, I am smothered by my enemy, I am beaten, I am scourged, I am killed, I am at the mercy of a lion, I am crushed in an oil press and my blood is squeezed out of me, I am hung, I am despised, I am exiled, I am in torment . . ."

At the end of his poem, there is a vision of the coming of the Messiah, the return of Elijah, and the restoration of Jerusalem and the Temple with its daily offerings.

What began in Blois spread throughout France from which, in 1306, all Jews were expelled.

They were, as Gersonides reckoned in a remark in his commentary on the Pentateuch, "twice the number that emerged from Egypt."

18

Alfonso X of Castile had decreed in the *Siete Partidas:* "Force and
   violence should not in any way be used on any Jew in order
   to convert him to Christianity. On the contrary Christians
   should convert them to the faith of our Lord Jesus Christ
   by good example, quotations from the Holy Scriptures and
   friendly persuasion. For Christ does not want or love any
   service which is done on his behalf by force."

But that changed. You can't persuade the Jews if they won't listen
   to your arguments. Enforced attendance at harangues was
   mandated for Jews. And if they remained unpersuaded and
   unconverted? If they persisted in willful ignorance? If they
   were perverse and, in Aquinas's formulation, unnatural, like
   homosexuals and lepers? What then?

A few Jews might have been accommodated. But with the Recon-
   quista, there were a lot of them. There were nasty stories
   about conspiracies in which lepers poisoned wells with pulver-
   ized host, pieces of snakes and toads, and human excrement,
   all of which had been given to them by Jews at the behest
   of the Sultan of Babylonia. And there were stories of ritual
   murders, the Blood Libel.

In Seville, in June 1391, there was a massacre of Jews. And then in
   Cordoba and Toledo and Valencia. This was the great pogrom,
   the beginning of the end.

In 1470, the question was put to Judah Benardut: "Why do you
   not become a Christian? You are dejected, you are subjected,
   you are humiliated by any child. This is insufferable. This
   one throws stones at you. The other calls you a Jewish dog.

If you turned Christian, you would be honored, you could be obeyed, you could get offices and a thousand other honors."

Benardut's reply was brave but curiously Christian: "I hold fast to my religion and I believe that I will be saved in it, and the more humiliations I have to endure to sustain my religion the more shall my soul be saved."

The Edict of Expulsion of the Jews from Spain was signed in Granada on March 30, 1492, and promulgated to Castile and Aragon in late April. It charged that the Jews "always endeavor in every way they can to subvert our holy Catholic faith and to make faithful Christians withdraw and separate themselves from them, and attract and pervert them to their injurious opinions and belief, instructing them in the ceremonies and observances of their religion, holding meetings where they read and teach them what they are to believe and observe according to their religion; seeking to circumcise them and their children; giving them books from which they may read their prayers; and explaining to them the fasts they are to observe; assembling with them to read and to teach them the histories of their law, notifying to them the festivals previous to their occurring, and instructing them what they are to do and observe thereon; giving and carrying to them from their houses unleavened bread, and meat slaughtered with ceremonies; instructing them what they are to refrain from . . . in food as in other matters, for the due observance of their religion, and persuading them all they can to profess and keep the law of Moses."

The Jews had until July 31 — Tish'a b'Av — either to convert to Christianity or to depart from "our said kingdoms and dominions, with their sons, daughters, man-servants, maid-servants,

49

and Jewish attendants, both great and small, of whatever age they may be; and they shall not presume to return to, nor reside therein, nor in any part of them, either as residents, travelers, or in any other manner whatsoever, under pain that if they do not perform and execute the same . . . they incur the penalty of death and confiscation of their property to our treasury."

Fifty thousand families fled, or, as others say, fifty-three thousand, which would be a quarter of a million persons. Other estimates range between one hundred- and eight hundred thousand. Half of them went to Portugal, where they imagined they could wait out this unpleasantness and return to Spain when the troubles were past. Don Vidal bar Benveniste del Cavalleria had struck a bargain with the King of Portugal in which the Jews paid one ducat for every soul and a fourth part of all the merchandise they carried in order to be allowed into his country for a stay of six months' duration.

Others crossed to Oran or to Fez in Morocco, where there was a famine so intense that many Jews went into the city to sell their children for a loaf of bread. It is said, however, that the king of Fez was a kindly man, and when the famine was over, he ordered that anyone who had bought a Jewish child had to return him to his parents. Many of these Jews returned to Spain.

From the north, some Jews went to England, France, or Flanders. Others crossed into Navarre and Catalonia, from which they sailed to Italy and Turkey.

An informer in Venice in 1617 reported that he had seen Portuguese Jews there keeping the fast of "Thesabão when Jerusalem was destroyed by Titus and Vespasian."

Many of those who stayed were the Crypto-Jews, who continued to observe as well as they could the religion they had publicly forsworn. For generations, they avoided work and travel on the Sabbath. They avoided pork and shellfish. And they fasted on St. Ann's day, which is July 31.

19

It was as if time had stopped. The Second Temple was destroyed in 70, and the canon of the Bible was codified at Yavneh in about 100, and from then on, it seemed that the prophets had no more to say — or, worse, that God had no more to say or even to do. What could he do that he had not done already? The Romans? The Crusaders? The Inquisition? Cossacks? Nazis? Only change their hats and they are familiar enough, Assyrians, Edomites, or Egyptians.

And thus it will be, they believed, until the Messiah comes. Meanwhile, the Jews were to listen as if to the nearly inaudible mumbling of an old man, confused and often repeating himself, forgetful of details, but still loving, still wise, the one for whom and through whom they lived.

They tried, as they still do, to understand what he means and how he means it, even to the point of adopting his own slips and confusions, the wrong names for faces and places. But the point of the stories is clear enough, and their truths are precious,

For evil is evil, as obvious as gravity, and enslavement and death do not change, whether the tormentors' helmets be pointed or round, embellished with crests or plain.

The Jews read the same scroll year after year, rewinding it for Simchas Torah and starting again, when, "In the beginning God made the heavens and the earth." Wonderful, yes, but repetitive, obsessive, even catatonic. And what goes on outside the shul is of no account and cannot be allowed to affect the drone of the chanting.

It is a taste of that time after time when the Messiah will come, for each Sabbath brings with it a morsel of the sweet respite of that longed-for timelessness in the week's portion that comes around as surely as the earth revolves around the sun and the stars spin in the sky, marking the heavens with vowel points and cantilation marks the angels know how to read.

That relief for which we yearn is not only for us the living but even for the dead who are, for that day each week, excused from their torments as their angel-keepers are also excused from their duties of inflicting punishment.

In God's own time, this perfection will come, but until then we languish, waiting, and we curse not God but time, the burden of which we bear, but from which we have contrived to turn away, seeking refuge in prayer.

Year after year, generation after generation, it was always the same. But the expulsion from Spain was different, worse than what the English had done or the French, because this was not the first but seemed at the time to be the last of the purges. It looked to be the end of the life of the Jews in Europe.

20

Of the Shoah, what can one say? The Shoah is said to be the defining event for modern Judaism. But if we concede that to be case, then there is no reason in the universe, no law, no order. Man is wolf to man, and there is no God. Hitler wins.

There were 380,567 Jews in Warsaw at the outbreak of the war, thirty percent of the city's population. It was the greatest concentration of Jews in Europe.

From Abraham Lewin's diary: "22 July [1942]—the Day before Tish'a b'Av. A day of turmoil, chaos and fear: the news about the expulsion of Jews is spreading like lightning through the town, Jewish Warsaw has suddenly died, the shops are closed, Jews run by, in confusion, terrified. The Jewish streets are an appalling sight—the gloom is indescribable. There are dead bodies at several places. No one is counting them and no names are being given in this terrifying catastrophe. The expulsion is supposed to begin today from the hostels for the homeless and from the prisons. There is also talk of an evacuation of the hospital. Beggar children are being rounded up into wagons. I am thinking about my aged mother—it would be better to put her to sleep than to hand her over to those murderers.

"23 July—Tish'a b'Av. Disaster after disaster, misfortune after misfortune. The small ghetto has been turned out on to the streets . . . Rain has been falling all day. Weeping. The Jews are weeping. They are hoping for a miracle. The expulsion is continuing. Buildings are blockaded . . . On Zamenhof Street the Germans pulled people out of a tram and killed them on the spot.

"I can recall the stories told by Josephus. If we compare them with the slaughter committed by the Germans in our times, then I come to the conclusion that the Germans' deeds today are more bloody, more vicious and more shocking than those of the Greeks and Romans 2,000 years ago. We must not forget that then there was a struggle; today unarmed and innocent people are being brutally killed. And what is more—since then, nearly 19 centuries have passed, and it is 153 years since the French Revolution and the declaration of the rights of man."

From Rabbi Kalonymus Kalmish Shapiro's penultimate sermon from his home on 5 Dzielna Street, which was now also a synagogue and soup kitchen: "God is not punishing the Jews in this attack, but rather, he is, himself, the object of the attack. Jewish suffering, no matter how great, is less than his. It comes not through Israel's fault but Israel's virtue and close ties with the almighty."

This is perhaps comforting, but not enough. We cannot bring those people back. Or their world. Or their faith. And there are some who wouldn't want to. That faith—that we are the Chosen People—they see as the gentile's warrant for our persecution.

There is a midrash on Lamentations in which Moses upbraids God, saying, "Lord of the Universe, you have written in your Torah, 'Whether it be a cow or a ewe, you shall not kill it and its young both in one day,'* but they have killed many, many mothers and sons, and you are silent."

God's answer to Moses, if he had one, is not recorded.

* Leviticus 22.28

55

Moshe-Leyb Halpern had seen it coming. He had written twenty
years before:

> A drayhorse comes, as white as snow
> Pulling a wagon with nothing in it.
> Icicles of blood hang from its muzzle,
> and diamonds of ice gleam in its mane.

21

They answer each other somehow, the Temple and Auschwitz, for
   if one was the place where God was present, the other was the
   place from which he was absent.

But the smell in the air of burning flesh would have been much
   the same. The offerings of cattle and sheep on God's table
   must have filled the air with an awful sweetness—there were
   220,000 oxen and 120,000 sheep in Solomon's grisly rite*—
   that would not have been unlike what drifted through the air
   from the crematoria's chimneys.

Grief at the loss of the Temple is what has shaped our thoughts
   and judgments. From the Temple Mount as surely as from
   Sinai comes the word of the Lord that we have taken to heart.
   Its wound is painful but perhaps that pain is better than the
   lack of all feeling. It is at any rate in our broken-heartedness
   at the ruin of the Temple and its city that we have lived for
   millennia, exiles, estranged, strangers.

Our first loss was of Eden, which may be said to have figured all
   other disasters. The many destructions of Jerusalem were
   confirming catastrophes. In our grief there was a wisdom we
   acquired—or it acquired us. It made us what we are, yearning
   for relief but no longer expecting it.

In our distress, we remade our religion and ourselves, for our woe
   had taken us beyond David's lyric flights and Solomon's wisdom to the awful truths of the world God made. Our tears,
   we come to understand, are also in His image.

* 1 Kings 8.63

After the ruin of the Temple, we could never again be surprised—
not even by Auschwitz.

PART II

Lamentations

אֵיכָה

| יֵשְׁבָה בָדָד הָעִיר רַבָּתִי עָם
הָיְתָה כְּאַלְמָנֶה רַבָּתִי בַגּוֹיִם
שָׂרָתִי בַּמְּדִינוֹת הָיְתָה לָמַס.

בָּכוֹ תִבְכֶּה בַּלַּיְלָה וְדִמְעָתָהּ עַל לֶחֱיָהּ
אֵין־לָהּ מְנַחֵם מִכָּל־אֹהֲבֶיהָ
כָּל־רֵעֶיהָ בָּגְדוּ בָהּ הָיוּ לָהּ לְאֹיְבִים.

גָּלְתָה יְהוּדָה מֵעֹנִי וּמֵרֹב עֲבֹדָה
הִיא יֵשְׁבָה בַגּוֹיִם לֹא מָצְאָה מָנוֹחַ
כָּל־רֹדְפֶיהָ הִשִּׂיגוּהָ בֵּין הַמְּצָרִים.

דַּרְכֵי צִיּוֹן אֲבֵלוֹת מִבְּלִי בָּאֵי מוֹעֵד
כָּל־שְׁעָרֶיהָ שׁוֹמֵמִין כֹּהֲנֶיהָ נֶאֱנָחִים
בְּתוּלֹתֶיהָ נּוּגוֹת וְהִיא מַר־לָהּ.

הָיוּ צָרֶיהָ לְרֹאשׁ אֹיְבֶיהָ שָׁלוּ
כִּי־יהוה הוֹגָהּ עַל־רֹב פְּשָׁעֶיהָ
עוֹלָלֶיהָ הָלְכוּ שְׁבִי לִפְנֵי־צָר.

וַיֵּצֵא מִן בַּת־צִיּוֹן כָּל־הֲדָרָהּ
הָיוּ שָׂרֶיהָ כְּאַיָּלִים לֹא־מָצְאוּ מִרְעֶה
וַיֵּלְכוּ בְלֹא־כֹחַ לִפְנֵי רוֹדֵף.

1

Alas, a woman, widowed, alone, the city sits that once was full of
people and great among the nations, a princess among the
provinces, now turned tributary.

Bereft, she weeps in the night, her bitter tears trailing down her
cheeks. Of her many lovers none is left to console or comfort.
Her friends have forsaken her now and become the friends of
her foes.

Captive is Judah, in servitude sorely afflicted. A lady once, the equal
of any, she is lowly now like a servant who cannot rest; her
oppressor persecutes her in her time of torment.

Desolate, Zion's roads are empty now and in mourning. No travelers come on feast days. Her gates are lonely, abandoned. Her
priests groan and her maidens, sobbing, are dragged away.

Enemies prosper and foes triumph: the Lord has afflicted her for
her many transgressions. Her children are carried away, her
conqueror's prizes and captives.

From the daughter of Zion all beauty is banished and glory is gone.
Her princes are starving deer that are lacking in speed and
strength and cannot elude their pursuers.

זָכְרָה יְרוּשָׁלַ֙͏ִם יְמֵ֣י עָנְיָהּ֙ וּמְרוּדֶ֔יהָ
כֹּ֚ל מַחֲמֻדֶ֔יהָ אֲשֶׁ֥ר הָי֖וּ מִ֣ימֵי קֶ֑דֶם
בִּנְפֹ֧ל עַמָּ֣הּ בְּיַד־צָ֗ר וְאֵ֤ין עוֹזֵר֙ לָ֔הּ
רָא֣וּהָ צָרִ֔ים שָׂחֲק֖וּ עַל־מִשְׁבַּתֶּֽהָ׃

חֵ֤טְא חָֽטְאָה֙ יְר֣וּשָׁלַ֔͏ִם עַל־כֵּ֖ן לְנִידָ֣ה הָיָ֑תָה
כָּֽל־מְכַבְּדֶ֤יהָ הִזִּיל֙וּהָ֙ כִּֽי־רָא֣וּ עֶרְוָתָ֔הּ
גַּם־הִ֥יא נֶאֶנְחָ֖ה וַתָּ֥שָׁב אָחֽוֹר׃

טֻמְאָתָ֣הּ בְּשׁוּלֶ֗יהָ לֹ֤א זָֽכְרָה֙ אַחֲרִיתָ֔הּ
וַתֵּ֣רֶד פְּלָאִ֔ים אֵ֥ין מְנַחֵ֖ם לָ֑הּ
רְאֵ֤ה יְהוָה֙ אֶת־עָנְיִ֔י כִּ֥י הִגְדִּ֖יל אוֹיֵֽב׃

יָדוֹ֙ פָּ֣רַשׂ צָ֔ר עַ֖ל כָּל־מַחֲמַדֶּ֑יהָ
כִּֽי־רָאֲתָ֣ה גוֹיִם֙ בָּ֣אוּ מִקְדָּשָׁ֔הּ
אֲשֶׁ֣ר צִוִּ֔יתָה לֹא־יָבֹ֥אוּ בַקָּהָ֖ל לָֽךְ׃

כָּל־עַמָּ֤הּ נֶאֱנָחִים֙ מְבַקְשִׁ֣ים לֶ֔חֶם
נָתְנ֧וּ מַחֲמַדֵּיהֶ֛ם בְּאֹ֖כֶל לְהָשִׁ֣יב נָ֑פֶשׁ
רְאֵ֤ה יְהוָה֙ וְהַבִּ֔יטָה כִּ֥י הָיִ֖יתִי זוֹלֵלָֽה׃

ל֣וֹא אֲלֵיכֶם֮ כָּל־עֹ֣בְרֵי דֶרֶךְ֒ הַבִּ֣יטוּ וּרְא֔וּ
אִם־יֵ֤שׁ מַכְאוֹב֙ כְּמַכְאֹבִ֔י אֲשֶׁ֥ר עוֹלַ֖ל לִ֑י
אֲשֶׁר֙ הוֹגָ֣ה יְהוָ֔ה בְּי֖וֹם חֲר֥וֹן אַפּֽוֹ׃

מִמָּר֛וֹם שָֽׁלַח־אֵ֥שׁ בְּעַצְמֹתַ֖י וַיִּרְדֶּ֑נָּה
פָּרַ֤שׂ רֶ֙שֶׁת֙ לְרַגְלַ֔י הֱשִׁיבַ֣נִי אָח֔וֹר
נְתָנַ֙נִי֙ שֹֽׁמֵמָ֔ה כָּל־הַיּ֖וֹם דָּוָֽה׃

נִשְׂקַ֞ד עֹ֤ל פְּשָׁעַי֙ בְּיָד֔וֹ יִשְׂתָּרְג֖וּ
עָל֣וּ עַל־צַוָּארִ֑י הִכְשִׁ֥יל כֹּחִ֖י
נְתָנַ֣נִי אֲדֹנָ֔י בִּידֵ֖י לֹא־אוּכַ֥ל קֽוּם׃

Gone are all the good times that Jerusalem cannot remember, those pleasant and prosperous days before her townsfolk fell into the enemy's hands and none was there to help her. Her adversaries gloated and mocked her desolation.

How grievously has Jerusalem sinned: she is filthy, unclean, and all that did her honor have seen her naked and shamed. She groans in the grief she feels and turns away her face.

Impurity hid in the hems of her skirts, but she took no heed. Her fall is all the worse for she herself was at fault, and no one cares or comforts. "O Lord," she cries, "behold my woe, for my foe has triumphed."

Jackboots have marched in the temple where barbarous hands have besmirched the sacred objects and fouled the holy places where fear and respect should have kept them away.

Keening and sighing, her people search for crusts of bread; jewels they trade for meat in their frailty and famine. "See, O Lord, how far I am fallen, to what I'm reduced."

Look, all you who pass, and see if you have a sorrow that is anything like my sorrow in the day of the Lord's great wrath.

My bones burn with the hot fire he hurled upon me. He spread a net to entangle my feet. He has checked my steps and has left me stunned and faint at the end of the dismal day.

Now is the yoke of my sins that the Lord has woven together heavy upon my neck. I stagger beneath their weight. The Lord has delivered me over into my enemies' hands, and I cannot stand against them.

סִלָּ֨ה כָל־אַבִּירַ֤י | אֲדֹנָי֙ בְּקִרְבִּ֔י
קָרָ֥א עָלַ֛י מוֹעֵ֖ד לִשְׁבֹּ֣ר בַּחוּרָ֑י
גַּ֤ת דָּרַךְ֙ אֲדֹנָ֔י לִבְתוּלַ֖ת בַּת־יְהוּדָֽה׃

עַל־אֵ֣לֶּה | אֲנִ֣י בוֹכִיָּ֗ה עֵינִ֣י | עֵינִי֮ יֹ֣רְדָה מַּ֒יִם֒
כִּֽי־רָחַ֥ק מִמֶּ֛נִּי מְנַחֵ֖ם מֵשִׁ֣יב נַפְשִׁ֑י
הָי֤וּ בָנַי֙ שֽׁוֹמֵמִ֔ים כִּ֥י גָבַ֖ר אוֹיֵֽב׃

פֵּֽרְשָׂ֨ה צִיּ֜וֹן בְּיָדֶ֗יהָ אֵ֤ין מְנַחֵם֙ לָ֔הּ
צִוָּ֧ה יְהֹוָ֛ה לְיַעֲקֹ֖ב סְבִיבָ֣יו צָרָ֑יו
הָיְתָ֧ה יְרוּשָׁלַ֛͏ִם לְנִדָּ֖ה בֵּינֵיהֶֽם׃

צַדִּ֥יק ה֛וּא יְהֹוָ֖ה כִּ֣י פִ֣יהוּ מָרִ֑יתִי
שִׁמְעוּ־נָ֣א כָל־הָ֣עַמִּ֗ים וּרְאוּ֙ מַכְאֹבִ֔י
בְּתוּלֹתַ֥י וּבַחוּרַ֖י הָלְכ֥וּ בַשֶּֽׁבִי׃

קָרָ֤אתִי לַֽמְאַהֲבַי֙ הֵ֣מָּה רִמּ֔וּנִי
כֹּהֲנַ֥י וּזְקֵנַ֖י בָּעִ֣יר גָּוָ֑עוּ
כִּֽי־בִקְשׁ֥וּ אֹ֙כֶל֙ לָ֔מוֹ וְיָשִׁ֖יבוּ אֶת־נַפְשָֽׁם׃

רְאֵ֨ה יְהֹוָ֤ה כִּֽי־צַר־לִי֙ מֵעַ֣י חֳמַרְמָ֔רוּ
נֶהְפַּ֤ךְ לִבִּי֙ בְּקִרְבִּ֔י כִּ֥י מָר֖וֹ מָרִ֑יתִי
מִח֥וּץ שִׁכְּלָה־חֶ֖רֶב בַּבַּ֥יִת כַּמָּֽוֶת׃

שָׁמְע֞וּ כִּ֧י נֶאֱנָחָ֣ה אָ֗נִי אֵ֤ין מְנַחֵם֙ לִ֔י
כָּל־אֹ֨יְבַ֜י שָׁמְע֤וּ רָֽעָתִי֙ שָׂ֔שׂוּ כִּ֥י אַתָּ֖ה עָשִׂ֑יתָ
הֵבֵ֥אתָ יוֹם־קָרָ֖אתָ וְיִֽהְי֥וּ כָמֹֽנִי׃

תָּבֹ֨א כָל־רָעָתָ֤ם לְפָנֶ֙יךָ֙ וְעוֹלֵ֣ל לָ֔מוֹ
כַּאֲשֶׁ֥ר עוֹלַ֛לְתָּ לִ֖י עַ֣ל כָּל־פְּשָׁעָ֑י
כִּֽי־רַבּ֥וֹת אַנְחֹתַ֖י וְלִבִּ֥י דַוָּֽי׃

Our mighty men are trampled and trodden underfoot. The Lord
has assembled foes to crush our fearless fighters. And our
maidens he has ground down, all the daughters of Judah, as if
they were gathered grapes dumped down into a winepress.

Piteous are these things, and I weep and my eyes stream tears; the
comforter that should soothe my soul is far away. My children, in desolation, see that my enemy wins.

Quavering hands does Zion hold forth, requiring comfort, but there
is none to console or offer her any aid, for the Lord has filled
her neighbors' hearts with implacable hatred: Jerusalem, once
fair, is foul as a piece of filth.

Rebellion against the Lord is what I have rashly raised, and the Lord
is right to chastise me. The world sees how I suffer. My maidens and my young men are banished and sent into bondage.

Seeking food for their empty bellies, my priests and my elders have
perished throughout the city. I have called out to my lovers,
but they have been false and have failed me.

That I am in deep distress, O Lord, you can surely see: my bowels
are troubled; my heart is sore and sickens within me. I have
behaved badly, and everywhere there are swords dealing death
abroad, and at home, too, there is death.

Up to now, there was none to comfort me or care. My enemies
heard of my trouble and delighted at what you have done. But
one day, you will visit your wrath upon them, too, and they
shall know your anger and be as bereft as I am.

Visit upon their transgressions the punishment you have inflicted
on me in my moment of pain, for I see how they are wicked
and my faith fights with despair. The sighs of my soul are
many and my heavy heart is faint.

יָעִיב בְּאַפּוֹ | אֲדֹנָי אֶת־בַּת־צִיּוֹן
הִשְׁלִיךְ מִשָּׁמַיִם אֶרֶץ תִּפְאֶרֶת יִשְׂרָאֵל
וְלֹא־זָכַר הֲדֹם־רַגְלָיו בְּיוֹם אַפּוֹ.

בִּלַּע אֲדֹנָי וְלֹא חָמַל אֵת כָּל־נְאוֹת יַעֲקֹב
הָרַס בְּעֶבְרָתוֹ מִבְצְרֵי בַת־יְהוּדָה
הִגִּיעַ לָאָרֶץ חִלֵּל מַמְלָכָה וְשָׂרֶיהָ.

גָּדַע בָּחֳרִי־אַף כֹּל קֶרֶן יִשְׂרָאֵל
הֵשִׁיב אָחוֹר יְמִינוֹ מִפְּנֵי אוֹיֵב
וַיִּבְעַר בְּיַעֲקֹב כְּאֵשׁ לֶהָבָה אָכְלָה סָבִיב.

דָּרַךְ קַשְׁתּוֹ כְּאוֹיֵב נִצָּב יְמִינוֹ
כְּצָר וַיַּהֲרֹג כֹּל מַחֲמַדֵּי־עָיִן
בְּאֹהֶל בַּת־צִיּוֹן שָׁפַךְ כָּאֵשׁ חֲמָתוֹ.

הָיָה אֲדֹנָי | כְּאוֹיֵב בִּלַּע יִשְׂרָאֵל
בִּלַּע כָּל־אַרְמְנוֹתֶיהָ שִׁחֵת מִבְצָרָיו
וַיֶּרֶב בְּבַת־יְהוּדָה תַּאֲנִיָּה וַאֲנִיָּה.

וַיַּחְמֹס כַּגַּן שֻׂכּוֹ שִׁחֵת מֹעֲדוֹ
שִׁכַּח יְהוָה | בְּצִיּוֹן מוֹעֵד וְשַׁבָּת
וַיִּנְאַץ בְּזַעַם־אַפּוֹ מֶלֶךְ וְכֹהֵן.

זָנַח אֲדֹנָי | מִזְבְּחוֹ נִאֵר מִקְדָּשׁוֹ
הִסְגִּיר בְּיַד־אוֹיֵב חוֹמֹת אַרְמְנוֹתֶיהָ
קוֹל נָתְנוּ בְּבֵית־יְהוָה כְּיוֹם מוֹעֵד.

חָשַׁב יְהוָה | לְהַשְׁחִית חוֹמַת בַּת־צִיּוֹן
נָטָה קָו לֹא־הֵשִׁיב יָדוֹ מִבַּלֵּעַ
וַיַּאֲבֶל־חֵל וְחוֹמָה יַחְדָּו אֻמְלָלוּ.

2

Alas, the cloud of the Lord has darkened the daughter of Zion; his anger has cast down Israel's beauty from heaven. On the day of his wrath, he does not remember his footstool.

Battering Judah's strongholds, the Lord has leveled the habitations of Jacob. In fury, he has brought low the king and the kingdom and ground its rulers into the dirt.

Cutting down in his rage Israel's might, he has withdrawn his right hand from them as they face their foe. He has burned like a bright fire in Jacob, consuming everything everywhere.

Death he has brought to all that was good for the eye to behold. He has bent his bow against us and set his right hand to shoot. He has poured forth his fury's fire into the tent of the daughter of Zion.

Enmity he has shown us: our mourning and lamentation are multiplied. He has become an enemy, destroying Israel, razing its palaces and ruining its fortresses.

Feasts and Sabbaths in Zion the Lord has ended; in his wrath he has spurned both king and priest. He has struck his tabernacle like a farmer's garden shed and has turned the place of his feasts into desolation.

God has rejected his altar and spurned his sanctuary. He has turned the walls of Zion's palaces over to the enemy. There was clamor and consternation in the house of the Lord on the appointed feast day.

He has levied a line of troops against the daughter of Zion. He has not stayed his hand but is intent on destruction. He has made the ramparts and walls weep as they languish together.

טָבְעוּ בָאָרֶץ שְׁעָרֶיהָ אִבַּד וְשִׁבַּר בְּרִיחֶיהָ
מַלְכָּהּ וְשָׂרֶיהָ בַגּוֹיִם אֵין תּוֹרָה
גַּם־נְבִיאֶיהָ לֹא־מָצְאוּ חָזוֹן מֵיהֹוָה.

יֵשְׁבוּ לָאָרֶץ יִדְּמוּ זִקְנֵי בַת־צִיּוֹן
הֶעֱלוּ עָפָר עַל־רֹאשָׁם חָגְרוּ שַׂקִּים
הוֹרִידוּ לָאָרֶץ רֹאשָׁן בְּתוּלֹת יְרוּשָׁלִָם.

כָּלוּ בַדְּמָעוֹת עֵינַי חֳמַרְמְרוּ מֵעַי
נִשְׁפַּךְ לָאָרֶץ כְּבֵדִי עַל־שֶׁבֶר בַּת־עַמִּי
בֵּעָטֵף עוֹלֵל וְיוֹנֵק בִּרְחֹבוֹת קִרְיָה.

לְאִמֹּתָם יֹאמְרוּ אַיֵּה דָּגָן וָיָיִן
בְּהִתְעַטְּפָם כֶּחָלָל בִּרְחֹבוֹת עִיר
בְּהִשְׁתַּפֵּךְ נַפְשָׁם אֶל־חֵיק אִמֹּתָם.

מָה־אֲעִידֵךְ מָה אֲדַמֶּה־לָּךְ הַבַּת יְרוּשָׁלִַם
מָה אַשְׁוֶה־לָּךְ וַאֲנַחֲמֵךְ בְּתוּלַת בַּת־צִיּוֹן
כִּי־גָדוֹל כַּיָּם שִׁבְרֵךְ מִי יִרְפָּא־לָךְ.

נְבִיאַיִךְ חָזוּ לָךְ שָׁוְא וְתָפֵל
וְלֹא־גִלּוּ עַל־עֲוֹנֵךְ לְהָשִׁיב שְׁבוּתֵךְ
וַיֶּחֱזוּ לָךְ מַשְׂאוֹת שָׁוְא וּמַדּוּחִים.

סָפְקוּ עָלַיִךְ כַּפַּיִם כָּל־עֹבְרֵי דֶרֶךְ
שָׁרְקוּ וַיָּנִעוּ רֹאשָׁם עַל־בַּת יְרוּשָׁלִָם
הֲזֹאת הָעִיר שֶׁיֹּאמְרוּ כְּלִילַת יֹפִי מָשׂוֹשׂ לְכָל־הָאָרֶץ.

Into the ground, her gates are sunk. The Lord has broken her for-
tifications. Her king and her princes are scattered among the
nations. The law is suspended and prophets wait for word
from the Lord.

Just like men in mourning, the elders of Zion sit on the ground
in silence with dust and ashes on their heads and wearing the
sackcloth of sorrow. The maidens of Jerusalem mourn and
hang their heads in grief.

Knees weak, eyes full of tears, and even my bowels bothered, I am
sick with grief for the city's wreck and my people's ruin as I
see our sorry children and even suckling babes collapse in the
desolate streets.

Like wounded men, they stagger and fall in the thoroughfares.
They cry to their mothers for something to eat and drink, as
they die on their desperate mothers' laps or at their dismayed
bosoms.

My mind is numbed. What can I say to you? How can I comfort,
O daughter of Jerusalem? To what can I compare your dreadful griefs, O maiden of Zion? Your ruin is vast, as deep as the
sea, irreparable and beyond any consolation.

Now, where are those prophets with their vain visions and fool-
ish predictions? They did not guess your guilt or prevent
your captivity. They said the useless things they thought you
wanted to hear.

On the road, passers-by shake their heads and hiss in derision or
laugh at Jerusalem's dismal daughter. They ask one another,
"Is this the city men have called the perfection of beauty? Was
this what they all spoke of as the joy of the whole world?"

פָּצוּ עָלַיִךְ פִּיהֶם כָּל־אֹיְבַיִךְ
שָׁרְקוּ וַיַּחַרְקוּ־שֵׁן אָמְרוּ בִּלָּעְנוּ
אַךְ זֶה הַיּוֹם שֶׁקִּוִּינֻהוּ מָצָאנוּ רָאִינוּ.

עָשָׂה יהוה אֲשֶׁר זָמָם בִּצַּע אֶמְרָתוֹ
אֲשֶׁר צִוָּה מִימֵי־קֶדֶם הָרַס וְלֹא חָמָל
וַיְשַׂמַּח עָלַיִךְ אוֹיֵב הֵרִים קֶרֶן צָרָיִךְ.

צָעַק לִבָּם אֶל־אֲדֹנָי חוֹמַת בַּת־צִיּוֹן
הוֹרִידִי כַנַּחַל דִּמְעָה יוֹמָם וָלַיְלָה
אַל־תִּתְּנִי פוּגַת לָךְ אַל־תִּדֹּם בַּת־עֵינֵךְ.

קוּמִי | רֹנִּי בַלַּיְלָה לְרֹאשׁ אַשְׁמֻרוֹת
שִׁפְכִי כַמַּיִם לִבֵּךְ נֹכַח פְּנֵי אֲדֹנָי
שְׂאִי אֵלָיו כַּפַּיִךְ עַל־נֶפֶשׁ עוֹלָלַיִךְ
הָעֲטוּפִים בְּרָעָב בְּרֹאשׁ כָּל־חוּצוֹת.

רְאֵה יהוה וְהַבִּיטָה לְמִי עוֹלַלְתָּ כֹּה
אִם־תֹּאכַלְנָה נָשִׁים פִּרְיָם עֹלְלֵי טִפֻּחִים
אִם־יֵהָרֵג בְּמִקְדַּשׁ אֲדֹנָי כֹּהֵן וְנָבִיא.

שָׁכְבוּ לָאָרֶץ חוּצוֹת נַעַר וְזָקֵן
בְּתוּלֹתַי וּבַחוּרַי נָפְלוּ בֶחָרֶב
הָרַגְתָּ בְּיוֹם אַפֶּךָ טָבַחְתָּ לֹא חָמָלְתָּ.

תִּקְרָא כְיוֹם מוֹעֵד מְגוּרַי מִסָּבִיב
וְלֹא הָיָה בְּיוֹם אַף־יהוה פָּלִיט וְשָׂרִיד
אֲשֶׁר־טִפַּחְתִּי וְרִבִּיתִי אֹיְבִי כִלָּם.

70

Proudly, your enemies rail; they whistle and jeer, exulting: "See how
we have destroyed her! This is the day we dreamed of, and we
have survived to see it."

Quite precisely, the Lord has done what he threatened to do and
long ago ordained. He has ruined you altogether. Your enemies
he has exalted and made them all rejoice.

Rivers of tears stream down our faces. Cry aloud to the Lord,
O daughter of Zion. Without pause or respite, weep in
remorse and grieve.

Stand up before the Lord; pour out your hearts to him. Lift your
hands for the sake of your children who faint in hunger and
die on the streetcorners. From one watch to the next, cry, cry
out all night long.

That women crazed by hunger should eat their own children,
that prophets and priests should be slain in the sanctuary's
safety . . . Is this your work, O God? Do you see what is hap-
pening here? Is this what you could have wanted?

Under the sun, the bodies of young men and of old lie in the dust
of the streets. My brave youths and my lovely maidens are
slain by the sword. In the day of your awful anger, you have
slaughtered them mercilessly.

Victims we are, who thought we were guests at the sacrifice. Instead
we witness terrors and undergo them ourselves. None has es-
caped or survived. The babies I dandled and reared I have seen
my enemy slaughter.

אֲנִי הַגֶּ֗בֶר רָאָ֣ה עֳנִי֮ בְּשֵׁ֣בֶט עֶבְרָתֽוֹ.
אוֹתִ֥י נָהַ֛ג וַיֹּלַ֖ךְ חֹ֥שֶׁךְ וְלֹא־אֽוֹר.
אַ֣ךְ בִּ֥י יָשֻׁ֛ב יַהֲפֹ֥ךְ יָד֖וֹ כָּל־הַיּֽוֹם.

בִּלָּ֤ה בְשָׂרִי֙ וְעוֹרִ֔י שִׁבַּ֖ר עַצְמוֹתָֽי.
בָּנָ֥ה עָלַ֛י וַיַּקַּ֖ף רֹ֥אשׁ וּתְלָאָֽה.
בְּמַחֲשַׁכִּ֥ים הוֹשִׁיבַ֖נִי כְּמֵתֵ֥י עוֹלָֽם.

גָּדַ֧ר בַּעֲדִ֛י וְלֹ֥א אֵצֵ֖א הִכְבִּ֥יד נְחָשְׁתִּֽי.
גַּ֣ם כִּ֤י אֶזְעַק֙ וַאֲשַׁוֵּ֔עַ שָׂתַ֖ם תְּפִלָּתִֽי.
גָּדַ֤ר דְּרָכַי֙ בְּגָזִ֔ית נְתִיבֹתַ֖י עִוָּֽה.

דֹּ֣ב אֹרֵ֥ב הוּא֙ לִ֔י אֲרִ֖יה בְּמִסְתָּרִֽים.
דְּרָכַ֥י סוֹרֵ֛ר וַֽיְפַשְּׁחֵ֖נִי שָׂמַ֥נִי שֹׁמֵֽם.
דָּרַ֤ךְ קַשְׁתּוֹ֙ וַיַּצִּיבֵ֔נִי כַּמַּטָּרָ֖א לַחֵֽץ.

הֵבִיא֙ בְּכִלְיוֹתָ֔י בְּנֵ֖י אַשְׁפָּתֽוֹ.
הָיִ֤יתִי שְּׂחֹק֙ לְכָל־עַמִּ֔י נְגִינָתָ֖ם כָּל־הַיּֽוֹם.
הִשְׂבִּיעַ֥נִי בַמְּרוֹרִ֖ים הִרְוַ֥נִי לַעֲנָֽה.

וַיַּגְרֵ֤ס בֶּֽחָצָץ֙ שִׁנָּ֔י הִכְפִּישַׁ֖נִי בָּאֵֽפֶר.
וַתִּזְנַ֧ח מִשָּׁל֛וֹם נַפְשִׁ֖י נָשִׁ֥יתִי טוֹבָֽה.
וָאֹמַר֙ אָבַ֣ד נִצְחִ֔י וְתוֹחַלְתִּ֖י מֵיהוָֽה.

זְכָר־עָנְיִ֥י וּמְרוּדִ֖י לַעֲנָ֥ה וָרֹֽאשׁ.
זָכ֣וֹר תִּזְכּ֔וֹר וְתָשׁ֖וֹחַ עָלַ֥י נַפְשִֽׁי.
זֹ֛את אָשִׁ֥יב אֶל־לִבִּ֖י עַל־כֵּ֥ן אוֹחִֽיל.

3

Afflicted am I and beset, a man whom God in his wrath has abased. Abused by his rod and broken, I am driven into the darkness. Against me, he turned his hand, and again and again.

Bones broken, wasted, I am besieged and battered. Bitterness is my portion and tribulation. Banished, I dwell in the darkest darkness like those who are long dead.

Chained so I cannot escape and walled in, I am a captive. Crying for help, I call out, but he will not hear my prayer. Crooked are all my paths, which he has blocked with boulders.

Desolate am I and desperate, and he lies in wait like a bear in his den or a lurking lion. Detours I must walk to avoid the many dangers. Desperate I am and defenseless, as he aims all his arrows at me.

Everyone everywhere laughs and all my people mock me. Even into my heart he shoots the arrows of his anger. Each day fills me with bitterness and feeds me with foul wormwood.

Forgetting what happiness is, I grind my teeth on gravel and cover myself in ashes. Fretful, my soul is tormented and knows no time of peace. Flown is all my glory; forsaken am I by the Lord.

Gall and wormwood are all I know, and the bitterness of a soul bowed down. Grief is my constant portion, and I am laid low and ruined. Gone are my many hopes, and sorrow is my sole companion.

חַסְדֵי יהוה כִּי לֹא־תָמְנוּ כִּי לֹא־כָלוּ רַחֲמָיו.
חֲדָשִׁים לַבְּקָרִים רַבָּה אֱמוּנָתֶךָ.
חֶלְקִי יהוה אָמְרָה נַפְשִׁי עַל־כֵּן אוֹחִיל לוֹ.

טוֹב יהוה לְקֹוָו לְנֶפֶשׁ תִּדְרְשֶׁנּוּ.
טוֹב וְיָחִיל וְדוּמָם לִתְשׁוּעַת יהוה.
טוֹב לַגֶּבֶר כִּי־יִשָּׂא עֹל בִּנְעוּרָיו.

יֵשֵׁב בָּדָד וְיִדֹּם כִּי נָטַל עָלָיו.
יִתֵּן בֶּעָפָר פִּיהוּ אוּלַי יֵשׁ תִּקְוָה.
יִתֵּן לְמַכֵּהוּ לֶחִי יִשְׂבַּע בְּחֶרְפָּה.

כִּי לֹא יִזְנַח לְעוֹלָם אֲדֹנָי.
כִּי אִם־הוֹגָה וְרִחַם כְּרֹב חֲסָדָו.
כִּי לֹא עִנָּה מִלִּבּוֹ וַיַּגֶּה בְּנֵי־אִישׁ.

לְדַכֵּא תַּחַת רַגְלָיו כֹּל אֲסִירֵי אָרֶץ.
לְהַטּוֹת מִשְׁפַּט־גֶּבֶר נֶגֶד פְּנֵי עֶלְיוֹן.
לְעַוֵּת אָדָם בְּרִיבוֹ אֲדֹנָי לֹא רָאָה.

מִי זֶה אָמַר וַתֶּהִי אֲדֹנָי לֹא צִוָּה.
מִפִּי עֶלְיוֹן לֹא תֵצֵא הָרָעוֹת וְהַטּוֹב.
מַה־יִּתְאוֹנֵן אָדָם חָי גֶּבֶר עַל־חֲטָאָו.

נַחְפְּשָׂה דְרָכֵינוּ וְנַחְקֹרָה וְנָשׁוּבָה עַד־יהוה.
נִשָּׂא לְבָבֵנוּ אֶל־כַּפָּיִם אֶל־אֵל בַּשָּׁמָיִם.
נַחְנוּ פָשַׁעְנוּ וּמָרִינוּ אַתָּה לֹא סָלָחְתָּ.

סַכֹּתָה בָאַף וַתִּרְדְּפֵנוּ הָרַגְתָּ לֹא חָמָלְתָּ.
סַכֹּתָה בֶעָנָן לָךְ מֵעֲבוֹר תְּפִלָּה.
סְחִי וּמָאוֹס תְּשִׂימֵנוּ בְּקֶרֶב הָעַמִּים.

How can the steadfast love of the Lord come to an end? How can the new day break and his endless mercies fail? Hope, I shall somehow cling to and remember how to say, "The Lord is my portion."

It is proper that one should be patient. In torment, one learns to wait in the Lord's good time for salvation. I know it can be better for a man to have borne the yoke in his youth.

Jeers one must learn to endure, and insults and even blows. Justification one dreams of when they crush his mouth in the dust. Just wait, he thinks, and he hopes that there yet may be reason to hope.

Keep faith, and try to believe that the Lord has not cast out forever the people he once kept close. Kindness and his compassion must conquer at long last. Kinfolk, meanwhile, grieve, and the sons of men are afflicted.

Lord, how can you allow that the weak be thus crushed underfoot? Let us not, in your presence, be thus beset and ruined. Lift up the hearts of those who long ago learned to love you.

Might it be that things come to pass without the will of the Lord? Must not his mouth ordain all good and evil events? Men ought never complain but accept the rebuke of the Lord.

Never lose faith but look to examine your ways and your people's. Now, even now, let us lift up our hands and our hearts to the Lord. Nod in acceptance and know that we have not yet been forgiven.

Obscured as the sun is obscured by a cloak of clouds, you hide: our prayers cannot get through. Oppressing us with your anger, you are unrelenting and kill us. Offal and refuse we are, and rejected by all the peoples.

פָּצוּ עָלֵינוּ פִּיהֶם כָּל־אֹיְבֵינוּ.
פַּחַד וָפַחַת הָיָה לָנוּ הַשֵּׁאת וְהַשָּׁבֶר.
פַּלְגֵי־מַיִם תֵּרַד עֵינִי עַל־שֶׁבֶר בַּת־עַמִּי.

עֵינִי נִגְּרָה וְלֹא תִדְמֶה מֵאֵין הֲפֻגוֹת.
עַד־יַשְׁקִיף וְיֵרֶא יהוה מִשָּׁמָיִם.
עֵינִי עוֹלְלָה לְנַפְשִׁי מִכֹּל בְּנוֹת עִירִי.

צוֹד צָדוּנִי כַּצִּפּוֹר אֹיְבַי חִנָּם.
צָמְתוּ בַבּוֹר חַיָּי וַיַּדּוּ־אֶבֶן בִּי.
צָפוּ־מַיִם עַל־רֹאשִׁי אָמַרְתִּי נִגְזָרְתִּי.

קָרָאתִי שִׁמְךָ יהוה מִבּוֹר תַּחְתִּיּוֹת.
קוֹלִי שָׁמָעְתָּ אַל־תַּעְלֵם אָזְנְךָ לְרַוְחָתִי לְשַׁוְעָתִי.
קָרַבְתָּ בְּיוֹם אֶקְרָאֶךָּ אָמַרְתָּ אַל־תִּירָא.

רַבְתָּ אֲדֹנָי רִיבֵי נַפְשִׁי גָּאַלְתָּ חַיָּי.
רָאִיתָה יהוה עַוָּתָתִי שָׁפְטָה מִשְׁפָּטִי.
רָאִיתָה כָּל־נִקְמָתָם כָּל־מַחְשְׁבֹתָם לִי.

שָׁמַעְתָּ חֶרְפָּתָם יהוה כָּל־מַחְשְׁבֹתָם עָלָי.
שִׂפְתֵי קָמַי וְהֶגְיוֹנָם עָלַי כָּל־הַיּוֹם.
שִׁבְתָּם וְקִימָתָם הַבִּיטָה אֲנִי מַנְגִּינָתָם.

תָּשִׁיב לָהֶם גְּמוּל יהוה כְּמַעֲשֵׂה יְדֵיהֶם.
תִּתֵּן לָהֶם מְגִנַּת־לֵב תַּאֲלָתְךָ לָהֶם.
תִּרְדֹּף בְּאַף וְתַשְׁמִידֵם מִתַּחַת שְׁמֵי יהוה.

Panic is all about us with pitfalls under our feet. Pitiless are our foes
    who persecute and insult us. People die, and my eyes that have
    seen such a series of horrors pour forth rivers of tears at the
    death and devastation.

Quavering voices of dying women I hear, and I weep. Quadruple and
    quintuple is my complaint to the Lord, who looks down
    and must hear. Quiet, as bad, follows, heartbreaking and
    deathly, as the echoes exhaust themselves.

Rounded up, like beasts, we are flung down deep into pits. Roughly
    they use us and hurl down stones on our helpless heads. Ruin,
    like waves of water, flows over us and drowns us.

Still, from the depths of that pit do I call on my Lord for help.
    So many times you have helped me; do not abandon me now.
    Strength and courage you gave me; give it again, O God.

Take up my cause, O Lord, as you have before, and save me. Terrible
    wrongs are done me: judge if this be unfair. Their vengeance
    and all their spite turn back and inflict it upon them.

Unspeakable things they have done, unbearable hurt and unendur-
    able insult. Until the end of the day and beyond, they speak
    against me and sing. Unceasing are their assaults.

Vanquish them, Lord, with your hands and requite their evil deeds.
    Vainglorious, vicious, vile, they deserve your curses upon
    them. Vigilant, you will pursue them, and from heaven destroy
    them forever.

אֵיכָה

יוּעַם זָהָב יִשְׁנֶא הַכֶּתֶם הַטּוֹב
תִּשְׁתַּפֵּכְנָה אַבְנֵי־קֹדֶשׁ בְּרֹאשׁ כָּל־חוּצוֹת.

בְּנֵי צִיּוֹן הַיְקָרִים הַמְסֻלָּאִים בַּפָּז
אֵיכָה נֶחְשְׁבוּ לְנִבְלֵי־חֶרֶשׂ מַעֲשֵׂה יְדֵי יוֹצֵר.

גַּם־תַּנִּים חָלְצוּ שַׁד הֵינִיקוּ גּוּרֵיהֶן
בַּת־עַמִּי לְאַכְזָר כַּיְ°עֵנִים בַּמִּדְבָּר.

דָּבַק לְשׁוֹן יוֹנֵק אֶל־חִכּוֹ בַּצָּמָא
עוֹלָלִים שָׁאֲלוּ לֶחֶם פֹּרֵשׂ אֵין לָהֶם.

הָאֹכְלִים לְמַעֲדַנִּים נָשַׁמּוּ בַּחוּצוֹת
הָאֱמֻנִים עֲלֵי תוֹלָע חִבְּקוּ אַשְׁפַּתּוֹת.

וַיִּגְדַּל עֲוֹן בַּת־עַמִּי מֵחַטַּאת סְדֹם
הַהֲפוּכָה כְמוֹ־רָגַע וְלֹא־חָלוּ בָהּ יָדָיִם.

זַכּוּ נְזִירֶיהָ מִשֶּׁלֶג צַחוּ מֵחָלָב
אָדְמוּ עֶצֶם מִפְּנִינִים סַפִּיר גִּזְרָתָם.

חָשַׁךְ מִשְּׁחוֹר תָּאֳרָם לֹא נִכְּרוּ בַּחוּצוֹת
צָפַד עוֹרָם עַל־עַצְמָם יָבֵשׁ הָיָה כָעֵץ.

טוֹבִים הָיוּ חַלְלֵי־חֶרֶב מֵחַלְלֵי רָעָב
שֶׁהֵם יָזֻבוּ מְדֻקָּרִים מִתְּנוּבוֹת שָׂדָי.

יְדֵי נָשִׁים רַחֲמָנִיּוֹת בִּשְּׁלוּ יַלְדֵיהֶן
הָיוּ לְבָרוֹת לָמוֹ בְּשֶׁבֶר בַּת־עַמִּי.

78

4

All the gold has been dulled, its pure luster lost. And the precious gems are strewn stones in the streets.

Bright sons of Zion, worth their weight in gold and diamonds, are scattered too, like shards from a broken pot.

Cruel jackals are tender and give suck to their young. More cruel is the daughter of my people, who cares for her children less than an ostrich will in the wild.

Dirty, hungry, thirsty, the children complain and beg, but no one comes to their aid.

Everywhere ruin attends. Those who nibbled on dainties are starving and die, and they who lolled on purple cushions now lie on ash heaps.

For the daughter of my people the chastisement has been harsher than the punishment Sodom received. No enemy came against them. And they died cleanly and quickly.

Great princes we had, purer than snow, whiter than milk, handsome, more lovely than gems they would wear.

How they are changed. Their faces are blacker than soot. Their skin is wrinkled, rougher than weathered wood.

Inch by inch, they dwindled and died, the victims of hunger, wasting away. Those who were slain by the sword turned out to be lucky.

Jews, starving and crazed, have boiled their own children. Thus the depths of destruction of city and people.

כִּלָּה יהוה אֶת־חֲמָתוֹ שָׁפַךְ חֲרוֹן אַפּוֹ
וַיַּצֶּת־אֵשׁ בְּצִיּוֹן וַתֹּאכַל יְסֹדֹתֶיהָ.

לֹא הֶאֱמִינוּ מַלְכֵי־אֶרֶץ כֹּל יֹשְׁבֵי תֵבֵל
כִּי יָבֹא צַר וְאוֹיֵב בְּשַׁעֲרֵי יְרוּשָׁלָםִ.

מֵחַטֹּאות נְבִיאֶיהָ עֲוֹנֹת כֹּהֲנֶיהָ
הַשֹּׁפְכִים בְּקִרְבָּהּ דַּם צַדִּיקִים.

נָעוּ עִוְרִים בַּחוּצוֹת נְגֹאֲלוּ בַּדָּם
בְּלֹא יוּכְלוּ יִגְּעוּ בִּלְבֻשֵׁיהֶם.

סוּרוּ טָמֵא קָרְאוּ לָמוֹ סוּרוּ סוּרוּ אַל־תִּגָּעוּ
כִּי נָצוּ גַּם־נָעוּ אָמְרוּ בַּגּוֹיִם לֹא יוֹסִפוּ לָגוּר.

פְּנֵי יהוה חִלְּקָם לֹא יוֹסִיף לְהַבִּיטָם
פְּנֵי כֹהֲנִים לֹא נָשָׂאוּ וּזְקֵנִים לֹא חָנָנוּ.

עוֹדֵינָה תִּכְלֶינָה עֵינֵינוּ אֶל־עֶזְרָתֵנוּ הָבֶל
בְּצִפִּיָּתֵנוּ צִפִּינוּ אֶל־גּוֹי לֹא יוֹשִׁעַ.

צָדוּ צְעָדֵינוּ מִלֶּכֶת בִּרְחֹבֹתֵינוּ
קָרַב קִצֵּנוּ מָלְאוּ יָמֵינוּ כִּי־בָא קִצֵּנוּ.

קַלִּים הָיוּ רֹדְפֵינוּ מִנִּשְׁרֵי שָׁמָיִם
עַל־הֶהָרִים דְּלָקֻנוּ בַּמִּדְבָּר אָרְבוּ לָנוּ.

רוּחַ אַפֵּינוּ מְשִׁיחַ יהוה נִלְכַּד בִּשְׁחִיתוֹתָם
אֲשֶׁר אָמַרְנוּ בְּצִלּוֹ נִחְיֶה בַגּוֹיִם.

שִׂישִׂי וְשִׂמְחִי בַּת־אֱדוֹם יוֹשֶׁבֶת בְּאֶרֶץ עוּץ
גַּם־עָלַיִךְ תַּעֲבָר־כּוֹס תִּשְׁכְּרִי וְתִתְעָרִי.

תַּם־עֲוֹנֵךְ בַּת־צִיּוֹן לֹא יוֹסִיף לְהַגְלוֹתֵךְ
פָּקַד עֲוֹנֵךְ בַּת־אֱדוֹם גִּלָּה עַל־חַטֹּאתָיִךְ.

Kindling a fire in Zion, the Lord has been wrathful; he has poured out his wrath, wrecking the city's foundations.

Lords of the earth did not believe, or their subjects either, that a foe could breach our walls or enter our gates.

Mayhem, madness, murder: for the sins of the priests and the prophets. For them the blood of the righteous is spilled in the streets.

None could touch their robes as they wandered blindly about the city, so defiled had they been with blood of their brethren.

"Out! Away! Unclean!" men cried as they passed. Oh, among men they were outcasts and exiles among all the nations.

Priests will be shown no more honor, nor elders esteemed, for the Lord has scattered them all.

Quaking with fear we watched for the nation to come that would save us, but in vain, all in vain.

Ruin pursued us, relentless. Strange men dogged our steps in the streets, and our days were numbered.

Swifter than vultures, our foes are, faster than falcons that fly in the heavens. They lay in wait and chased us.

The breath of our life, the Lord's anointed, our king has been taken away. He, under whose protection we lived, is lost.

Uz and Edom rejoice and are glad. But the bitter cup shall pass to their lips to drain to the dregs. And they shall be drunk and be stripped to nakedness' shame.

Vices of Zion are punished; but you, O Edom, will see your sins one day be requited also.

זְכֹר יהוה מֶה־הָיָה לָנוּ הַבִּיטָה וּרְאֵה אֶת־חֶרְפָּתֵנוּ.

נַחֲלָתֵנוּ נֶהֶפְכָה לְזָרִים בָּתֵּינוּ לְנָכְרִים.

יְתוֹמִים הָיִינוּ וְאֵין אָב אִמֹּתֵינוּ כְּאַלְמָנוֹת.

מֵימֵינוּ בְּכֶסֶף שָׁתִינוּ עֵצֵינוּ בִּמְחִיר יָבֹאוּ.

עַל צַוָּארֵנוּ נִרְדָּפְנוּ יָגַעְנוּ וְלֹא הוּנַח־לָנוּ.

מִצְרַיִם נָתַנּוּ יָד אַשּׁוּר לִשְׂבֹּעַ לָחֶם.

אֲבֹתֵינוּ חָטְאוּ וְאֵינָם וַאֲנַחְנוּ עֲוֹנֹתֵיהֶם סָבָלְנוּ.

עֲבָדִים מָשְׁלוּ בָנוּ פֹּרֵק אֵין מִיָּדָם.

בְּנַפְשֵׁנוּ נָבִיא לַחְמֵנוּ מִפְּנֵי חֶרֶב הַמִּדְבָּר.

עוֹרֵנוּ כְּתַנּוּר נִכְמָרוּ מִפְּנֵי זַלְעֲפוֹת רָעָב.

נָשִׁים בְּצִיּוֹן עִנּוּ בְּתֻלֹת בְּעָרֵי יְהוּדָה.

שָׂרִים בְּיָדָם נִתְלוּ פְּנֵי זְקֵנִים לֹא נֶהְדָּרוּ.

בַּחוּרִים טְחוֹן נָשָׂאוּ וּנְעָרִים בָּעֵץ כָּשָׁלוּ.

זְקֵנִים מִשַּׁעַר שָׁבָתוּ בַּחוּרִים מִנְּגִינָתָם.

שָׁבַת מְשׂוֹשׂ לִבֵּנוּ נֶהְפַּךְ לְאֵבֶל מְחוֹלֵנוּ.

נָפְלָה עֲטֶרֶת רֹאשֵׁנוּ אוֹי־נָא לָנוּ כִּי חָטָאנוּ.

5

Remember, O Lord, what has happened; see our disgrace.

Our inheritance has been given over to strangers and our homes to aliens.

We are fatherless orphans. Or our mothers are grieving widows.

Landless now we must pay for our wood and our water.

We are shackled and yoked, driven like beasts, weary, and have no rest.

We hold out our hands to Egypt, beg bread from Assyria.

Our fathers sinned but are dead, and we bear the weight of their guilt.

We are ruled by the slaves of strangers, and no one can save us.

We forage for food at our peril; we wander in wilderness fearing swordsmen at every step.

Our skin is hot as a stove with the fever of famine.

Women in Zion are raped, and Judah's virgins violated.

Princes are hung by their hands. Elders are mocked and abused.

Young men grind at the mill and boys are laden like beasts.

The old men have left our gates. Our youths have forgotten their songs.

The joys of our hearts are erased, and our dancers are seated in mourning.

The crown on our heads has fallen. For this, for our sins, Oh, woe!

עַל־זֶה הָיָה דָוֶה לִבֵּנוּ עַל־אֵלֶּה חָשְׁכוּ עֵינֵינוּ.

עַל הַר־צִיּוֹן שֶׁשָּׁמֵם שׁוּעָלִים הִלְּכוּ־בוֹ.

אַתָּה יהוה לְעוֹלָם תֵּשֵׁב כִּסְאֲךָ לְדֹר וָדוֹר.

לָמָּה לָנֶצַח תִּשְׁכָּחֵנוּ תַּעַזְבֵנוּ לְאֹרֶךְ יָמִים.

הֲשִׁיבֵנוּ יהוה | אֵלֶיךָ וְנָשׁוּבָה חַדֵּשׁ יָמֵינוּ כְּקֶדֶם.

כִּי אִם־מָאֹס מְאַסְתָּנוּ קָצַפְתָּ עָלֵינוּ עַד־מְאֹד.

Our hearts are sick. Our eyes are dim with tears.

Jackals prowl Mount Zion, a ruin now and a wasteland.

But you, O Lord, you reign for ever and ever. Your throne endures
   to all generations.

Why do you forget us, forsake us? How long can this go on?

Restore us to you, O Lord, renew us, refresh us . . .

Or is this a final rejection? Can your anger endure forever?

Bibliographical Note

Among the books I have consulted are the following:

Bartoszewski, Wladislaw T., and Antony Polonsky, eds. *The Jews in Warsaw: A History.* Oxford: Basil Blackwell, 1991.

Borchsenius, Poul. *The Son of a Star.* London: George Allen & Unwin, 1960.

Elon, Amos. *A Blood-Dimmed Tide.* New York: Columbia University Press, 1997.

Elon, Amos. *Jerusalem: Battlegrounds of Memory.* New York: Kodansha, 1995.

Gitlitz, David M. *Secrecy and Deceit: The Religion of the Crypto-Jews.* Philadelphia: Jewish Publication Society, 1996.

Jacobs, Joseph. *The Jews of Angevin England.* London: David Nutt, 1893.

Josephus, Flavius. *The Works of Flavius Josephus.* Trans. Sir Roger L'Estrange. London: Richard Sare, 1709. There are, of course, more recent translations, including those of William Whiston (New York: Norton, 1999) and H. St. J. Thackeray (New York: Viking/Penguin, 1984).

Kedouri, Elie, ed. *Spain and the Jews.* London: Thames & Hudson, 1992.

Keller, Werner. *The Bible as History.* London: Hodder & Stoughton, 1980.

Lewin, Abraham. *A Cup of Tears: A Diary of the Warsaw Ghetto.* Trans. Anthony Polonsky. Oxford: Basil Blackwell, 1988.

Metzger, Bruce M., and Michael D. Coogan, eds. *The Oxford Companion to the Bible.* Oxford: Oxford University Press, 1993.

Neusner, Jacob. *Ancient Israel after Catastrophe: The Religious World View of the Mishnah.* Charlottesville: University Press of Virginia, 1983.

Neusner, Jacob. *Vanquished Nation, Broken Spirit.* Cambridge: Cambridge University Press, 1987.

Roskies, David, ed. *The Literature of Destruction: Jewish Responses to Catastrophe.* Philadelphia: Jewish Publication Society, 1989.

Roth, Cecil. *A History of the Jews in England.* Oxford: Oxford University Press, 1978.

Rubenstein, Richard L. *After Auschwitz.* 2d ed. Baltimore: Johns Hopkins University Press, 1992.

Scheindlin, Raymond P. *A Short History of the Jewish People.* New York: Macmillan, 1998.

Stokes, H. P. *A Short History of the Jews in England.* London: Macmillan, 1921.

Tovey, D'blossiers. *History of the Jews in England.* 1738; reprint ed., New York: Burt Franklin, 1967.

Werblowsky, Zwi, and Geoffrey Wigoder, eds. *The Oxford Dictionary of the Jewish Religion.* Oxford: Oxford University Press, 1997.

Yerushalmi, Yosef Hayim. *Zakhor.* Seattle: University of Washington Press, 1996.

Zlotowitz, Rabbi Meir. *Megillas Eichah: Lamentations/A New Translation.* New York: Mesorah Publications, 1976.